To · Sara

AGAINST ALL ODDS

A True Story, With the Names
Changed to Protect the Guilty

To my
Spiritual mom
Happy mother's
Day! Your smile
breaks yours
Sara

God Bless!

by Pastor Kimberly Daniels

AGAINST ALL ODDS

by Pastor Kimberly Daniels

Spread the Word Publishing
9197 Camshire Dr.
Jacksonville, FL 32244
904-908-4261

"Editorial services by Bookmakers USA"

ISBN #1-929097-05-0

DEDICATION

To the saints of Spoken Word Ministries at Steele and Blue, my brothers and sisters in the Lord who stood with us as God took us from a mess to a miracle. I thank God for Pastor Sirretta Williams, our staff and our demon-busting partners. Most of all, I thank God for my husband Danny and his unselfish attitude in releasing me to do the work of the Lord. And to my children—Michael, Faith, Elijah and Elisha—I release the inheritance of the Lord and proclaim that the curse is broken in Jesus' name.

I give special thanks to Bishop Harvey Robinson, Bob Larson, and Dr. C. Peter Wagner who were instrumental in launching me in my evangelistic ministry.

Lastly, I would like to give special recognition to Bishop George Bloomer. He spoke into my life for a brief moment and deposited a seed that has brought forth much fruit. He was the first one to teach me about the python spirit. This teaching opened the door for new realms in spiritual warfare in my life.

TABLE OF CONTENTS

FOREWORDS

Pastor Kim Daniels is a living miracle. What she is doing today is amazing, particularly in light of her wayward life before meeting Christ. Pastor Kim's deliverance ministry is a direct result of her own deliverance from the powers of darkness. Her story will inspire and encourage believers and ministers everywhere.

The Lord is raising up a multitude of ministers who have come through the jaws of hell and lived to tell of His grace. They have been prepared through experience to minister to others who are in bondage. Kim Daniels is such a minister. She is someone you should meet and know.

Your life will be transformed by this life-changing story. Pastor Kim is not your ordinary minister. Her passion for the lost and desire to see people set free is a testimony of God's grace that will surely inspire faith and courage in your heart. The Lord has given her a revelation of the spirit realm, and her testimony will help you understand the powers of darkness that we fight against before and after salvation.

Although the contents of this book may seem almost unbelievable at times, they are real. Whether or not you are familiar with the kinds of things shared by Pastor Kim, your eyes will be opened to the reality of sin and its consequences. But more important, you will gain a fresh glimpse at the reality of God's love and grace. You will see God's power to give victory—against all odds.

Apostle John Eckhardt
Crusaders Ministries
Chicago, Illinois

If you hate the devil, you will love *Against All Odds*. If you want the devil's works destroyed, this book will change your life.

The Lord has anointed Pastor Kim to uniquely intertwine historical facts, revelation knowledge, common sense, humor and personal experiences. Like no other author that I have read, she uses these to unmask the schemes of the devil.

Many Christians have begun a journey out of the kingdom of darkness, but have not fully entered into God's marvelous light. In order to complete blessings of the Lord's marvelous light, we must come completely out of the devil's darkness. In this ingenious spiritual warfare game plan, Pastor Kim lays out a prayerful and practical strategy for fully coming out of darkness—and getting the darkness fully out of us.

Many people do not even realize the darkness that is still influencing them. As Hosea 4:6 warns, they perish for lack of knowledge. This book yanks the covers off the bed of ignorance and deeply ingrained satanic causes and effects. Pastor Kim has exposed the devil—big time!

Kim Daniel's testimony illustrates the delivering power of God to bring us out of Babylon and then cast the contamination of Babylon out of us. After she was removed from the negative influence of her environment, she was still plagued with a battle on the inside. It was not until she came to know Jesus and receive the inheritance of deliverance that she became an overcomer.

Lazarus walked out of the darkness of death at the command of Jesus' voice. Despite this, forces attempted to keep him in bondage. It was not until Jesus took authority over these unseen forces that Lazarus was released to full life. In a similar way, it is time for the body of Christ to take off her grave clothes and rise to full freedom and deliverance. This deliverance must be more than a spiritual cliché—it must be reality.

I am extremely grateful to God for giving this book to Pastor Kim. I applaud her obedience in communicating the Lord's message about deliverances in the twenty-first century. He is using her to inform and transform those who formerly viewed spiritual warfare as weird or spooky. Warfare is real—and so is Kim!

Pastor Kirbyjon Caldwell
Windsor Village United Methodist Church
Houston, Texas

The Word of God says that a person who is faithful over a few things will be made the ruler over many. Pastor Kim has triumphed against all odds and God has made her a ruler and a leader among her peers. I encourage you to read what this God-fearing woman has to say. You will be blessed.

Dr. Wallace J. Sibley
Administrative Bishop
Southern New England States
Church of God

PREFACE

A Personal Message to Readers of this Book

TO MY BROTHERS AND SISTERS IN THE LORD:

As you read this book, I pray that the Lord will reveal His heart—and my heart—to you. Some of the stories that I tell may be hard to believe. In order to receive the fullness of what this book has to offer, you must shut down the voice of your natural man and test the spirit of this book by the Spirit of God.

My motive is to tell truths that will set captives free. The Bible says we will know each other by the fruit and by the love. I pray that the fruit of these words will cause the *agape* love of God to permeate your inner being.

As believers we have too often become critical of things we did not understand or agree with. I try to make it a practice not to judge that which I do not have a full understanding of. This practice has helped me maintain a level of deliverance that keeps my heart free from witchcraft. A *"kritikos"* (critical) spirit makes a clean heart dirty, and witchcraft flows fluently through dirty hearts.

Critical spirits and broken relationships must be speedily dealt with, as Jesus instructs us in Matthew 5:24-25:

> *Leave thy gift before the altar, and go thy way; first be reconciled to thy brother, and then come and offer thy gift. Agree with thine adversary quickly, while thou art in the way with him; lest any time the adversary deliver thee to the judge, and the judge deliver thee to the officer, and thou be cast into prison.*

The *kritikos* spirit is very common in the church, but often goes unrecognized. The accuser of the brethren has laid deadly traps that are snaring God's chosen vessels and leading them into bondage. I did not understand why God would ask us to agree with our adversary, especially when the Greek interpretation of that word means "satan." Why should we be quick to agree with satan?!

This word "agree" in the Greek is *eunoeo,* and it means to be "well minded." This scripture is actually telling us to have the right attitude when we go through challenges that are initiated by the evil one. We also have to be careful about our attitude toward those that the enemy may use to accomplish his purpose. Based on this scripture, we can see that whether we are right or wrong in a situation, we have no right to be bitter or resentful.

In Mary K. Baxter's book *A Divine Revelation of Hell,* she tells of a woman whose husband committed adultery. In the story, the woman who was cheated on went to hell. It would seem that the *violator* would be punished, but in this story the *victim* received the punishment. How could the husband commit adultery and the wife go to hell? The above scripture explains it all too well. Though he committed the adulterous act, she took on the demon, the spirit of the *kritikos*!

The man repented and turned from his evil ways, and God forgave him. The woman could never forgive her husband for his covenant-breaking act. She was a minister and was living right before the Lord. Not only did she have a hard time forgiving her husband, but she ultimately became mad at God for allowing this to happen to a "good Christian" such as herself. She eventually committed suicide. She was turned over to the "jailer."

When we have the wrong attitude about going through trials and tribulations, the adversary will turn us over to the judge, who is the critical spirit. The judge will then turn us over to the jailer, who is the spirit of bondage. The Bible says we must count it all joy when we fall into diverse trials. This is more than an option—it is a clear command. Failure to follow it will result in deep bondage.

It saddens my spirit when we are critical against one another because of differences of opinions. If 10 born-again believers close themselves in a room for a day, differences will begin to emerge. Differences are not always bad, and God often allows us to compliment each other in our differences (see 1 Cor. 12).

I have seen leaders in the body of Christ blackball other believers because of trifling differences. Jesus settled this kind of issue when the disciples questioned the work of a group that was not of their fold. This group was operating outside of the realm that the disciples were familiar with. They did not understand God using anyone outside of their 12-man clique.

Jesus dealt with them sternly and said, "If they are not against us, they are for us!" This immediately broke the "curse of the clique." This curse blinds the eyes of many Christians, hindering them from seeing that God can use people outside of their group. Operating under this deception opens the door to a familiar spirit called "the clique."

As you read this book, allow God to minister to you by His Spirit. I had to pay a great price to be able to write these words. I present this book to you as a gift from my heart, and I pray that you receive it in wisdom, in love and in joy.

TO THOSE ON THE OTHER SIDE

This message is also a warning to those who are knowingly serving satan and are willingly operating on the dark side of spirituality. I realize that there is an empty space inside you that torments your soul.

Some of you may have backslidden from the Lord because you were turned over to the critical spirit. The Bible says that God is married to the backslider. No matter how many hexes you have cast, you can be totally delivered. Any markings satan has placed on your physical body or on your very soul are not stronger than the blood of Jesus. No matter how dirty your hands have become while messing around with satan, the blood of Jesus will wash you as clean as snow.

Satan is a lowdown dog, and you know it! Turn in your gear from the dark side and lay it all down. No matter what your motives are for reading this book, the Holy Ghost wants to touch your life!

I love you,
Pastor Kim

Chapter 1
BEGINNINGS

I have received many prophecies concerning the call of God on my life. Not many years ago two women of God spoke into my life at a prophetic conference in central Florida. Prophetesses Sharon Stone and Cathy Lechner were probably not familiar with my ministry, but they prophesied life into that which had not yet been born concerning it.

The word of the Lord was that I would pastor a church in a neighborhood that had become a waste place. The prophetesses said that the church building would need a facelift and that God would supernaturally provide renovation. I was also told that people would travel from around the nation to come to this building and be delivered. They prophesied that God would spiritually and physically restore the entire neighborhood.

These words came to pass a few years ago when Bishops Quan Miller and Wallace Sibley of the Church of God gave me the keys to a building with an auditorium that seated 900. My only instructions were to turn the electricity on and have church! I had never seen the inside of the building until the first time I preached in it. The only time I had even been in the neighborhood was when I was taking a shortcut to work one day. The Holy Spirit prompted me to circle a vicinity of the neighborhood seven times. He told me on the last trip around to shout as loud as I could with the windows rolled down.

The area had a lot of drug traffic, and as I kept circling the area I began to draw the attention of the dealers. I am sure they thought I worked for the police. When on the last trip I shouted at the top of my voice, little did I know that my ministry would soon be within the perimeters of this small community. Hallelujah, when I shouted, the walls came down!

Getting permission to use the building was only the beginning. The area seemed virtually unreachable. The prostitutes and drug dealers had no respect for the house of God, and they would do business transactions right on the church steps. A dark cloud lingered overhead, and the building was actually haunted. We would have demonic attacks of pestilence, whereby we would be covered with bites from head to toe. During our worship services, the doors of the church would open and close without any assistance. The building was filled with a dead stench that no house cleaner could get rid of.

For two years we could count our visitors on one hand, and even Easter Sunday did not bring in a new face. We had four families, totaling 18 members if the children and teenagers were counted. Even as we believed God for an increase of our numbers, our four-family congregation dwindled down to two. Sirretta Williams joined our church, Spoken Word Ministries, and became my assistant pastor.

Among the Lepers

After a divorce, a church split, and the experience of standing before the "Sanhedrin" in my city, I knew what it was like to be in the midst of the twilight hour. When I think of the twilight hour, I remember the four lepers at the gate of Samaria, where there was a great famine (see 2 Kin. 7). During this time in my life, I felt like one of the lepers. There was no provision in my city, and if I stayed where I was I would surely die. My only alternative was to go to the enemy's camp. Satan had all my goods, and I refused to allow him to keep them.

The Bible says that the lepers "got up" and went toward the enemy's camp at the twilight hour. Whether people are serving God or not, everyone has experienced a fall in life at one time or another. The Word of God says a righteous man will fall seven times, but he can get up every time.

The lepers "got up" before it was too late. We wrestle not against flesh and blood (Eph. 6:12). In any wrestling match the goal of each opponent is to pin the other person down long enough to defeat them. The devil wants us to stay down for the count—but the lepers "got up"! The point I would like to address is not the significance of them getting up, but it was the timing in which they did so.

The highlight of the miracle was the synchronization of when the lepers moved and when God moved. The two things took place at the same time. On one hand, the lepers "got up" and moved toward the enemy's camp, with not even an inkling of victory. On the other hand, God sent a delusion to the enemy's camp that caused them to flee in fear. The result was a moving of all hindrances to God's provision.

The great thing about this miracle was that it not only blessed the ones who moved out in faith, it also impacted those in the city who were left behind holding the baggage. The Spirit of the Lord is seeking someone to stand in the gap. He is seeking someone who will share the spoils of victory with His people and cause the walls of the city to be rebuilt.

The lepers seemed like unlikely heroes, but it is just like God to use somebody who is not qualified. The Syrians thought that a mighty army was approaching them. It was only the sound of a few lepers "getting up"! Against all odds, the lepers gained the victory by risking their lives and obeying the Lord.

Life in the Twilight Hour

This all happened at the twilight hour. Twilight is the time when drastic change is about to take place. Jacob wrestled with the angel all night, but his breakthrough came at the crack of day. Until he could see the light, he held on to God all night long. When circumstances get darkest, those who know how to wait on Him will experience great breakthroughs! In the darkest hour, even the faintest crack of light seems wonderfully bright.

I'll be the first to admit that Spoken Word Ministries appeared to be in a leprous situation in those days. People are afraid to be around lepers, because they don't want the lepers' disease to rub off on them. All of Samaria was not leprous, but there was a famine in the city. Though the lepers had specific physical ailments, *everybody* was hungry! The entire city was in the twilight zone, but the lepers appeared to be worse off.

My city, Jacksonville, Florida, wasn't experiencing a famine of food, but a "deliverance famine." There was a shortage in the spirit of solid, ground-level deliverance ministry. Jacksonville has awesome ministries within its borders, but somehow the enemy crept in and put a bad taste in the mouths of the leaders for true demonic confrontation.

At Spoken Word we were willing to pay the price, but the enemy attempted to shut us down through various situations. Despite the challenges I faced, I never forgot the prophetic words that had been spoken over my life. I believed that the words of the prophets were tailor-made for me, and I held on with a death grip.

Sharon Stone spoke "Prophetic Evangelism" into my spirit, and I did not even understand the term. Not only did the Holy Spirit teach me what Prophetic Evangelism was, but today I flow fluently in the reality of it. Through the precision of the Holy Spirit's leading, we minister salvation, deliverance and healing to the nations.

As a church we withstood the storms during our early days in ministry. We escaped the snares of "Lilith" and moved into what God had called us to do. Lilith is the desert monster in the book of Isaiah. She is an avowed enemy of newborn babies and swears to kill them before one year. We have been very successful in breaking the power of crib death by dealing with this strongman. I believe that Lilith is also the spirit that is used to snuff out newborn churches. The first year of a church's existence is as delicate as the first year of a newborn baby's life. Spiritual crib death must be bound and dealt with severely. A similar demonic entity is "Lamia," the vampire spirit that aids abortion and miscarriage.

Transforming a Community

The word of the Lord did not fall to the ground. The community surrounding our church has been greatly renovated! The low-rent housing project was bulldozed to the ground. The crack houses were shut down. I am sure drug transactions still take place, but they are not as blatant.

The area around our ministry used to be called the Rat Bowl or Durkeville. It is now called The Oaks at Durkeville. The streets had potholes so deep that the front ends of cars could fall in, but now the city has completed a major maintenance project. The entire area has been beautified with palm trees.

For a while some dared to continue selling drugs on the church steps. But when people began to drop dead on the steps, this kind of ungodly action suddenly ceased. The dark cloud moved from our building, and the sun seemed to shine brighter than before.

We have witnessed the transformation of our community even though there has been very little organized evangelistic effort on our part. Our focus has been on intercession and personal witnessing. No organized street evangelism has taken place in our immediate area. It would seem feasible for us to invade the streets, since we have a church full of ex-street people. Yet this has not been according to our instructions from the Lord.

I am in no way attempting to lay a blueprint for every inner-city ministry. It is my strong conviction that what has worked for me may cause another to fail. The foundation of Spoken Word Ministries is our commitment to "Expanded Territorial Warfare." This level of territorial warfare is not limited to geographical location, but expands to a broader scope of consciousness of God's will for our everyday steps.

In the military this is called "attention to detail." A good soldier has no problem following orders at any cost. But to be able to follow orders, we must know what the orders are. To effectively operate in Expanded Territorial Warfare, we must know His voice. To know His voice, our "spiritual discerners" must be sharpened through consecration. We must separate ourselves from the unclean thing. Contamination clogs up our discerner and either distorts or shuts down our hearing.

One of the greatest causes of casualties in war is the failure of soldiers to pay attention to detail. The word of the Lord tells us that a little leaven leavens the whole lump, and the little foxes spoil the vine. The little things we overlook can often open doors to the evil one. When the word of God says, "Give no room to the devil," it means exactly that.

For the past three years we have been building a foundation and preparing to train the multitudes in warfare and deliverance. To tell the truth, we have spent the past three years *getting delivered!* The most important ingredient in deliverance ministry is first getting the pigs out of our own parlors. There is nothing like casting out devils and going to bed with a clear conscience at night. Our ministry is almost ready to target the streets, but we are waiting on orders from Jesus, our Commander in Chief.

This book is a testimony of how God delivered me from cocaine and the life of the streets. My prayer is that those who are called to minister the gospel will get a vision of its true power as they read my testimony. Escaping the spirits of *Pharmekia* and the Vampire spirit from the crack house was a miracle that only God could have performed.

However, I must admit that escaping the grips of Jezebel, Python and Leviathan in the church was much more challenging than being delivered from drugs. Though it is wonderful that I have been delivered from the demonic bondage of *"inner city,"* an even greater aspect of my testimony is that I have been delivered from the *"inner church."* Praise God, I have been delivered from being in a religious clique! Because of that, I am free to minister wherever God sends me.

The Prophecies of Satan

Just as God sent me prophetic words about my destiny, satan sent me lies and threats. One day a man called me from a local cult group that he identified as the Eifi. He explained to me that he was studying to become a voodoo priest. I later found out that this group was known as the Yoruba Religion.

Yoruba's foundation is based on the worship of ancestors. Many young musicians have tapped into the art of Yoruba to conjure the spirits of popular singing artists that have died. The following quote was taken from a prominent entertainment magazine:

21

D'Angelo recorded his long-awaited new album, *Voodoo* (Virgin), at Electric Lady Studio, which Jimi Hendrix built on Eight Street in Manhattan's Greenwich Village. The studio pet, a white cat named Jimi, would follow D'Angelo around and curl up in his lap while D' worked out some lyric or chord. And of course, he has nightmares about conjuring up Marvin Gaye. He was channeling the dirty mind the artist abandoned for Jehovah. But *Voodoo* isn't about them. It is about Grandmother and Grandfather. And tambourines. And the tarrying that goes on till four in the morning. Because sometimes it's slow-coming, baring one's soul. Becoming naked to God, vulnerable to the ancestors and their ancient tongues. Sometimes it takes three whole years of tarrying to call a spirit down (*Vibe* magazine, April 2000).

The above statement refers to a very popular pop artist today. The magazine cover refers to him as "casting soulful spells," and he is said to have blessed the public with his otherworldly album, *Voodoo*. The article cites the inspiration behind his music as growing up in the church, the birth of his son, and channeling souls. Yoruba is becoming a fad to the old and young, the rich and poor. Mixing voodoo and Catholicism, it draws those who have been looking for something "powerful" to be a part of. The temporary benefits appeal to many. They do not realize that these benefits are a one-way route to death.

The anonymous caller who was studying to become a voodoo priest of this group explained that he had been sending death curses against Pastor Bea and me. He divulged that their powers had not been working against us, and concluded that we were on the right track. Before he hung up the phone he told me that he wanted to leave the craft if he could find a sure way out. He also said very strongly to me, "Whatever you are doing…keep on doing it!"

The Death of a Mighty Warrior

As I think back on this phone call, it almost seems unreal. The only thing that testifies of the reality of his call is that Pastor Bea died of cancer a few months ago. Though we casually kept in contact, the enemy had slowly severed our relationship in ministry. The church community was devastated by her death. My mentor, demon-busting buddy, and dear sister in the Lord had gone home early.

Pastor Bea's death, at age 43, was one of the hardest things I had ever dealt with. For several days I did not leave my home. The devil had stolen one of my best friends. Pastor Bea is the one who prophesied that Spoken Word Ministries would come out of my belly. She named us demon busters and was the first one I heard yell, "Hey Ho, Devil, You Gotta Go!" I could never quite say those words like Pastor Bea. When she preached the gospel, the gates of hell trembled. Many were baffled about her early death. Only God knows the details, but we know that she fought the good fight of faith.

I dreamed about Pastor Bea six months before her death. We were preaching at an outdoor meeting, and I had the podium first. I began to address some demons very radically. After I finished talking, I passed the microphone to Pastor Bea. She quietly smiled and laid the microphone down. She looked at me and said, "I do not want to be involved." At that point she turned and boarded a helicopter that disappeared into the sky.

I did not have an understanding of the dream at the time, but it made me feel incredibly sad. A few months after this dream, I visited with Pastor Bea in a beauty salon. She never mentioned that she was sick, nor did she ask me to pray. We talked about going on the road and ministering together again. I was so excited to spend time with her that I never noticed the frailness of her body under the apron she wore.

Not long afterwards, Pastor Sirretta and I received a call to go and pray for Pastor Bea because she was dying. As I stood by the phone, allowing the reality to sink in, 30 minutes later Pastor Bea was dead! I never got a chance to pray for her. How could two people who were so close grow so far apart? Even unto death!

The words of the Eifi voodoo priest played over in my head. "Keep on doing whatever you are doing!" One of Pastor Bea's members joined my church. After we cast the devils out of her, she told us that she had never been through deliverance. She also stated that she had never witnessed a devil being cast out of anyone. How could this be? This young lady was with Pastor Bea for more than one year.

A Tribute to Pastor Bea

I know that I have at least one witness in heaven. As I write this book, my thoughts are often of her. She was an important part of my foundation in the Lord. Her godly lifestyle and instruction laid a blueprint in my life that is now building an effective ministry throughout the nation. One day we will fellowship again in heaven.

I miss Pastor Bea dearly, but as for now, I must continue my course. No matter what situation arises, I've got to keep doing what I have been called to do. I realize that it may cost me relationship with family and friends, but I must press toward the mark. We must all recognize and obtain what God has called us to do. As for me…I am called to cast out devils, and I will not settle for anything less.

No person, religion or foreign god can talk me out of my inheritance. The inheritance of a born-again believer has many unlimited promises, and I purpose to walk in all that God has for me. The revelation of God's Word has brought to my attention that certain aspects of our inheritance are in direct relationship to the glory of God's kingdom being released in the earthly realm.

While many seem preoccupied with praying "money cometh," my prayer is "kingdom cometh." The ironic thing is that if the kingdom comes, the money will come too. Jesus gave a specific guideline for our priorities when He told us to seek first the things of the kingdom of God, and all we have need of will be given to us (Matt. 6:33). The Bible clearly says that when we heal the sick and cast out devils...then the kingdom has come!

Chapter 2
SEASON OF 'THE LAST'

Well, I made it! Despite the hindrances and obstacles, I made it to Colorado Springs for the first National Congress on Deliverance Conference, organized by Dr. C. Peter Wagner. A spirit of expectancy was in the air. A new beginning was about to take place in my life.

I had never preached to a crowd or more than 500-600 people, and my heart was racing. Except for me, all the other speakers are familiar faces to those gathered. Just like when I ran in my first major track meet, I was the one without any accolades behind my name. Everyone was wondering, *Who is Kimberly Daniels?* Little did they know, I was wondering the same thing myself. Feeling like a nobody among so many bright and shining stars, I asked myself, *What am I doing speaking at a conference with some of the greatest spiritual warfare pioneers in the world?*

As thunder literally shook the building, I believe God was saying, "Yes, I approve of you! You aren't a nobody in my eyes!" The anointing fell in such a way that I was made a keynote speaker at the last minute. God had intervened in the planned agenda.

Can you grasp this amazing picture? An inner-city, 36-year-old, black female preacher was on the stage singing songs like, "Who Dat Trying to Be Bad," "Oops Up Side Yo Head," "We Go Cast the Devil Out" and "Tear the Roof Off the Sucker"— to a crowd of 3,000 believers. There were of course a few visitors from the "dark side" who got the shock of their lives. God was running things!

Thousands of people had demonic manifestations, followed by miraculous deliverances. Frowns turned to smiles, fear turned to faith, and minds that wandered began to tune into God. Out of it all, the Lord was getting the glory. Working in the background, my deliverance team went to another level of anointing as demons were tormented and cast out.

I call my deliverance team the dirty dozen, a name that aptly fitted the occasion. They are a group of 12 former prostitutes, drug addicts, homosexuals and even those from a Muslim background, all with a tremendous love for Jesus. What a picture their ministry at the conference presented: The church has been trying to get the inner city delivered, but in this case God brought the inner city to deliver the church!

While We Were Sleeping

Have you ever wondered what it meant when Jesus said the prostitutes would make heaven first? The types of bondage and addiction found in the inner city are so obvious that most of the people involved know they need help. A far worse situation is being in bondage and not knowing it. That's called deception.

The Bible says the enemy crept in and sowed evil seeds while the people of God slept (Matt. 13:25). This word "slept" in the Greek is *katheudo*, and it means to lie down and rest. Matthew mentions that demons seek resting places after they have been cast out. This is the same scripture that speaks of a wicked generation. I am afraid that this generation is not one that refuses to accept Christ, but one that continually reneges on their covenant with God. As a result, many become the resting places for demons, seven times worse than they were before. The word "wicked" used in this scripture is *poneros*, and it means to degenerate from original virtue. So I feel safe to say this refers to a backslidden condition where devils are multiplied seven times.

It has been a number of months since the Congress on Deliverance, but the lives of the ministers at Spoken Word Ministries will never be the same. The week after we ministered in Colorado Springs, we received calls from 40 states in two days. In one week, my speaking engagements were booked through December 2000. The taste of deliverance was in the mouths of the people at the conference, and spiritual warfare was in the air.

A year ago we sat, week after week, with 17 faithful members in a building that seats 900. At that point I could count the tapes we sold on one hand, but now our tapes are being sold around the world in record numbers. Not only am I myself getting requests to speak, but my deliverance teams are now ministering across the nation. When we sing one of our favorite praise songs, "Look What the Lord Has Done," it means so much more to us than before. I also know that the "fat lady" has not yet sung. The work God has begun, He will faithfully bring to fruition (Phil. 1:6).

My prayer is that ministers of the gospel will be encouraged through my testimony. My testimony is not that I have a church with 10,000 members. We presently have just 100 members on the home front. I know that God is a God of increase, but let's consider this: What is increase? I believe that increase is being in place to do what God has called us to do. In His perfect will, supernatural results come forth and only God gets the glory.

When something is refined, it is purged from all impurities. Quality has always outweighed quantity in importance, but if we put quality first, quantity will inevitably come too. My testimony had to be told while the church was small. People are bound to go looking for God in big things. The problem is, there is nothing big enough in the earthly realm to contain God. Elijah sought God in the big things but God was speaking to him through a still, small voice.

The Last Will Be First

I was excited to see that the most valuable player of the NFL Super Bowl in 2000 was Kurt Warner, who stocked grocery shelves for a living just a few years ago. We are living in the "season of the last." This is spoken of in the Gospels of Matthew and Mark, where Jesus says the last shall be first and the first shall be last. The word "last" in the Greek is *eschatos*, and it means "uttermost." Uttermost means "to the greatest degree possible." This is an encouraging word to those the enemy has oppressed or held down to demonic depths.

The Bible says a righteous man will fall down seven times, but will get up every time. Curses do not plague us when we fall down—only when we *stay* down. The Word of the Lord refers to our battle against dark forces as a wrestling match. The goal of the opponents in a wrestling match is to hold the opposition down "long enough." How long is long enough? This victory in wrestling only goes to those who endure to the end.

I get nervous when ministers tell me they *used to* cast out devils. The devil does not take a break! The word "rest" in Matthew 12:43 also refers to the fact that after devils have been cast out, they seek places that are taking an intermission from kingdom work. No matter where God takes me in ministry, I purpose to keep the devil under my feet.

The only way we can do this is to be seated in heavenly places (the third heaven) with Christ Jesus. The prince of the power of the air runs his air force from the second heaven. Either we pin him down or he will pin us down! To do this we must be strategically in place, seated with Christ.

Chapter 3
BATTLE STRATEGIES

Our team recently traveled to New Orleans to do a warfare conference. As we entered the plane, the stench of demons and the presence of witchcraft filled the atmosphere. Across from me sat a black man with stripes burned into his face and knots that looked like marbles in his head. I knew something was going on in the spirit: This was a doctor of voodoo.

At Spoken Word, we are called demon busters. This voodoo doctor meant business, and I knew we had to be demon busters or we would be busted! But I had new members traveling on my team, and I did not want to release fear on them. So I did what I do best—rapping warfare songs, out loud! Can you imagine a high-level witch doctor sitting on the plane next to a group singing "Oops Upside Your Head," "Who Dat Trying to Be Bad," and "Hey, Ho, Devil You Gotta Go"? We so tormented the devils in him that he jumped up and ran into the bathroom.

When we got to our hotel, supernatural manifestations were everywhere. The most astonishing thing was when birds started screaming and flapping from the inner walls of the hotel. The noise was unbearable. I immediately thought of Benson Idahosa's description in one of his books about how he dealt with birds sent by voodoo. Without thought, I said, "In the name of Jesus...die!" I never heard another sound from them.

The next morning, the Lord awakened me with an urgency to pray. I was praying with my face turned to the sofa and I began to smell the stench of sulfur. Before I could look around, something grabbed me. I could only see the hand, but I could tell it was an ectoplasm—the materialization of an astral body or spiritual entity. As this unseen force grabbed me I was quoting the scripture, *"Greater is he that is in me than he that is in the world!"* (1 Jn. 4:4)

This was not the attack of a nightmare spirit, for I was not sleeping. Nightmare spirits (often called "hanks," a witch riding a person) attack the physical body while the victim is asleep. The astral body (spirit of a person) is often conscious of the attack. Most of the people I have interviewed concerning this say that their spirit man began to call on Jesus and the unseen force released them.

Incubus and *Succubus* are other prominent nightmare spirits. Attacking people while they are sleeping, they promote perversion and lust. Often the victims will not discuss these types of occurrences, because either the enemy tricks them into believing it was only a dream or they are too embarrassed to discuss it.

Lessons from New Orleans

Although we successfully completed our mission in New Orleans, it was one of the most challenging ministry assignments we have ever had. I thank God for my athletic and military training. It often helps me when the Holy Spirit speaks to me concerning discipline and spiritual conditioning. Athletics, the military, and ministry have much in common in my life. I have always made an effort to be the best in whatever I set my mind to do, and this has been an important aspect of my service to God.

The Lord has used my natural training and background to help me devise the following formula for evangelism assignments:

ATHLETIC STANDPOINT	MILITARY STANDPOINT
1. Warm up	1. Preparation for battle
2. Competition	2. Activation of battle
3. Cool down	3. Deactivation of battle

Based on both of the above approaches, it can be easily understood that all three levels are essential elements for effective evangelism. They are defined as follows:

Level I - Getting combat-ready, assuring that all spiritual and physical requirements are met to support the battle vision.

Level II - Setting the vision in motion according to all that has been planned, always being open to the leading of the Holy Spirit.

Level III - Sealing the mission off from backlash and retaliation, making a conscious effort toward decontamination and closing all doors to a counterattack from the enemy.

Any military operation without effective "recon" and "decon" will ultimately end in disaster. These terms are military prefixes for *reconnaissance* and *decontamination* operations. These crucial elements of successful combat are defined as follows:

Reconnaissance - an exploration or inspection of an area for the purpose of gathering military information. In terms of spiritual warfare, this is often referred to as territorial mapping. Recon operations discern the territorial principalities over the area we have targeted for battle. The more precise we are in determining the satanic spirits involved, the more effective our engagement of battle will be.

Decontamination - to make safe by eliminating anything harmful that may have attached to us during the battle. The enemy will not take a vacation after our mission has been successfully carried out. "Post-military battle" is the most sensitive phase of combat. Many give the devil a black eye, but then lower their guards.

Some of the common strongmen we deal with in post-battle conflicts are:

1. Jezebel - After every great victory, this spirit comes to instill fear, as she did with the prophet Elijah.

2. Goon Spirits - These are bully spirits that seek to rob people of the Word immediately after they hear it.

3. Batman - This mind-blinding spirit, also referred to as the "hoodwink," tries to make a person think more of themselves than they ought to after God has used them.

The reason I am taking time to explain these phases of combat is because following this format has saved my life and the lives of those around me. Satan does not take kindly to those who enter the territories he has claimed as his. After witnessing great moves of God, I have seen such attacks as cancer, terminal illness against my children, and caging incantation against my staff. That's why many Christians choose to avoid spiritual warfare as much as possible—they don't want to deal with the fierce retaliation that will inevitably come from the enemy.

In Acts 20:22-23 (Amp), Paul clearly states:

> *And now, you see, I am going to Jerusalem, bound by the (Holy) Spirit, and obligated and compelled by the convictions of my own spirit, not knowing what will befall me there; expect that the Holy Spirit clearly and emphatically affirms to me that imprisonment and suffering await me.*

Paul said he did not have a choice, and I agree that no Christian should have one. Our lives are not our own. We cannot do whatever we please. Yes, in Christ we are more than conquerors, but the Bible also makes it clear that there are *conditions* to meet if we want to be overcomers: We must overcome by the blood of the Lamb, by the word of our testimony, and because we love not our lives unto death.

Facing the Backlash

I have encountered the devil's retaliation in my own life. After my experience with the voodoo doctor on the plane to New Orleans, my voice began to slowly deteriorate. At the same time, my youngest twin awakened in pain and could not walk. Because I was not feeling well myself, I stayed in bed while my husband took the child to the hospital. When they returned, it was with a report of nothing being found.

Pastor Sirretta and I knew that witchcraft was operating, and we sent it back to where it came from. Within a few minutes, my son was running around the house as normal. The next day I received a call from the medical expert at the hospital. They said they had found out what the problem was—an incurable disease that would cause his joints to deteriorate and keep him from ever walking again.

The peace of God was upon me as the doctor sadly gave his verdict, stating that my son's disease was ignited by a viral infection. I then asked the doctor whether, if his diagnosis was correct, could my son be running and playing. He responded that he could not. I joyfully told the doctor that Elisha was playing at full speed, tearing the house apart.

The doctor apologized and said the x-rays must have been wrong. I told him that the x-rays were right, but the devil just had the wrong one. Glory to God! Elisha was healed before we even received the diagnosis!

There is a spirit called "diagnosis." I am not saying all diagnoses are of the devil, but I have evidence that we must be prayerful concerning medical opinions. Through a ministry associate, I was informed that during a deliverance session a demon of infirmity refused to come out. The demon finally spoke through the person and said, "I do not have to come out because I have already been diagnosed!"

We have to be watchful of the spirit of *Nuhastan*. This is the snake that was wrapped around the pole that God allowed the people to look upon and be healed. From the time of Moses to Hezekiah, people continued to look to *Nuhastan* for healing, rather than to God. To this very day, the medical symbol is a pole with a snake coiled around it.

The danger in this is operating in vain repetitions. God will use people, places and things for a season, but the church easily takes its eyes off God and puts them on the particular mode He is using. This is why God-ordained revivals often continue after God's sanction has lifted. In the eyes of the people, they are still having revival. The truth of the matter is that they are entertaining familiar spirits, and the place is being ruled by the "other Jesus" spirit. In such situations, witchcraft spirits enter in and demonic manifestations begin to occur that people label as moves of the Holy Spirit.

Regaining My Voice

One month after our ministry trip to New Orleans, I was still having problems with my voice. In fact, it was continually growing worse. One night I received a call from a woman who had been a leader in 36 different cults. She has been delivered for 10 years now, but only discusses her prior lifestyle as the Holy Spirit leads. We will call her "Sister Free" for confidentiality purposes.

Sister Free said the Lord revealed to her that witches had pronounced viruses on my vocal chords. She stated that she had cursed the voices of many of God's people when she worked on the other side. Not only did she share the problem with me, but she also gave the solution. She told me some natural and spiritual steps to counteract the enemy's attack.

The woman said the attack on my voice was because the witches wanted to silence the "voice of John the Baptist" in my life. She explained that the witches claim this is why John the Baptist's head was cut off…to shut his mouth.

A few days later God gave me dreams and visions of sorcerers, voodoo doctors, and witches around the world who had voodoo dolls with mouths sewn up. Praise God, I broke the "curse that comes against the voice that cries out in the wilderness." My voice was restored. It was better than ever, and satan's minion was sent back to him for torment because he could not complete his mission.

By the way, the voodoo doctor on the plane came to me in a dream. He was on the plane telling me, "I am the man from the plane." His face appeared as a zombie. God had already told us to bind this spirit when we first encountered his presence. Sister Free said he came to deliver a curse while I was sleeping. She explained that some curses cannot be sent, but must be delivered. This is one of the main jobs of shamans, conjuring up fetishes in order to assign demons to objects so the objects will carry the curses.

Sister Free had been a shaman, studying to become a Cochina. In the dream the voodoo doctor took me to the plane door, opened it up, and showed me all that was his. When I looked down, there were beautiful islands, and all the buildings had large voodoo masks on the top of them. Before he offered me anything, I kicked him off the plane with my foot.

God really does have a sense of humor. The devil needs to know that this isn't just some horror movie—he's dealing with a real sister from the hood. One of my main strengths in the Lord is that I have no respect for evil.

In order for you to understand my ministry and what I am called to do, it will help if you understand what God has brought me out of. I pray that my testimony will be a blessing to all who read this book.

Chapter 4
Perilous Upbringing

The Bible says God knew Jeremiah before he was formed in his mother's womb, and that applies to us as well. However, just as God knows a person and is waiting for him to come forth and walk in his calling, the devil is waiting also. Revelation 12:4 talks about the great red dragon that was waiting as the woman travailed in labor, planning to devour her child as soon as he was born.

In a similar way, I realize that before I was born there were already some things stacked up against me. I was born in Jacksonville, Florida, in an area known to the local blacks as "uptown." Most people called it "downtown," but to us it was "uptown." My grandfather, grandmother, mother, aunt and two sisters all lived together in a wooden house on the corner of Beaver and Jefferson.

My grandmother, who was blind, met my grandfather in Raiford Prison on the chain gang. My grandfather was a professional thief and my grandmother was incarcerated for murder. My mother was somehow conceived during their incarceration according to my other aunt, Lillie Mae, who did not live with us. Lillie Mae always came to the rescue when havoc was wreaked in the house.

I don't remember much about my mother in my younger years except that she was attractive, tall, had big, pretty eyes, and she worked a lot. Everybody worked except my blind grandmother, so I got to stay home and help her. My Aunt Maude was the youngest of my mother's two sisters. She was very smart in school and went to college to become a nurse. This is the only job she ever had. She still has to this day: same job, same hospital, same Maude.

Maude was a lot like my grandmother—hard, mean and rarely showing emotions. She even cursed like my grandmother. She could cuss you out and the words would cut you to pieces. Out of everyone in my household, my grandfather and grandmother played major roles in the lives of my two sisters and me. I was older than my sisters, Thabathia and Sebrena.

Life With Grandmother

My grandmother was the authoritarian in the house, even though she had no eyes. She was not born blind, but in fact had 20/20 vision at one time. My grandmother had an extensive history with the police department for fighting, and she never did it unarmed. She and my grandfather originated from a small town called Madison, Florida, about 50 miles outside of Tallahassee. My Aunt Lillie Mae often told stories about how my grandmother and grandfather lived before we were born. Her father lived in Madison, and all I remember about him was his name "Poppa" and that his bathroom was outside the house in a shed.

My grandmother's mother was said to be some kind of tough woman. Tough, strong-minded women seem to run in our blood-line. My grandmother took the role of a gangster-type woman, and even in a time when blacks were expected to be soft-spoken to white people, she was boisterous, even against the police. I remember watching her pull her underwear down and turning her backside to the police, giving them an invitation for trouble. I'm sure they were not excited to take her invitation on.

My grandmother was a very large woman, and if she sat down with no bra on, her breast would cover her lap. She carried all kinds of things in the center of her bra, which she called her bosom. My grandmother stuffed her bosom with guns, knives, liquor bottles and even her peach snuff. Her name was Ms. Ella Mae Parrish, but we called her Big Momma.

Over and over again I would ask Aunt Lillie Mae to rehearse how Big Momma became blind, because the story seemed unbelievable. One of her eyes had no eyeball and was closed shut, and the other eyeball was such a grayish pale color that you could easily tell it did not work. Lillie Mae said Big Momma had a white boyfriend who was obsessed with her. He had purchased her a refrigerator, but when she did not act like he wanted her to, he came to take the refrigerator back.

Big Momma did not take too kindly to anyone taking something that she considered hers, so she started physically fighting with this man. The man picked up an ax and hit her across the forehead, cracking her skull and blinding her left eye. As a result of this, she had a metal plate put in her head. This is the man she later went to Raiford Prison for, after she blew his head off with a gun. She shot him not just once, but seven times—and she ended up serving a year in prison for each of those bullets.

We were told that my grandmother's sentence would have been longer if it had not been for the intervention of her uncle, who was involved with running whorehouses and gambling operations for the mafia in Chicago. My family's main illegal occupation had been dealing in moonshine, however, and my grandmother's moonshine operation had made her a woman of powerful influence in the community.

Later Big Momma married my grandaddy and they got in a horrible fight, which they did on a regular basis. My grandmother picked up an ice pick to swing at my grandfather and tripped and fell off the porch. The ice pick turned and plucked her eyeball completely out. The eyeball was hanging from the cord that connected it to the socket while it lay on her chest. In a fit of rage, my grandmother attempted to pull the eyeball by the cord completely out of her head, telling God, "Just take both of the #@*!" She cursed at God, telling Him that He might as well take both of her eyes. All this time, she did not realize she was talking to the "god of this world" (2 Cor. 4:4).

The Fruit of Bitterness

My grandmother was a very bitter woman. Even though she loved us, she had a strange way of showing it. She would curse me out like a sailor and hug me at the same time. No one physically disciplined us except her, not even my mother or grandfather. She had a great influence on my early life—but it was not a good influence.

Because of my grandmother's handicap, I was her eyes and hands. I saw and did all that she could not see and do. She drank Smirnoff Vodka, dipped peach snuff, used Noxzema skin cream, drank the short-bottled coca cola, and chewed Juicy Fruit gum. Whenever she needed something, I was the one she called to get it.

I will never forget her spit can. This was usually an empty coffee can that she spit her snuff into. Often she would kick it over or drop it, and guess who had to clean it up! The smell and the look of it were so gross, it would spoil my appetite.

Ms. Ella Mae would often tell me parts of the Bible. She often talked about Jesus coming back and the end times. She was the first one I heard tell of the creature that would sting people during the tribulation, so they would seek death and not be able to find it. She also spoke of a time that was coming when we would not be able to buy or sell. Despite her references to the Bible, her lifestyle did not reflect Jesus at all. She cursed so often that I learned cussing as a second language. Though English was my first language, the second was cursing.

The murdering spirit that operated in my grandmother's life was not limited to outsiders. My grandfather went to the emergency room many nights because of attempts on his life by my grandmother. I will never forget the time she made me walk up to him, leading her by the hand—and she slit his chest wide open. The blood sprinkled onto my face. I was only six years old at the time.

During this same time period, my grandmother would constantly accuse my grandfather of having affairs with other women. Though she was blind, she would often tell me of two women she knew he was sleeping with. One time she made me lead her up to one of the ladies at a bar. We lived in an apartment house over the bar at the time. Grandmother briefed me on how to lead her up to the lady and then back away.

Though I was crying on the inside, I dared not let a peep or whimper escape, because Ms. Ella would never allow that. As grandmother walked up to the lady, she pulled a switchblade from her bra and put it to the lady's throat. Though she threatened the woman, she did not kill her. It must not have been that lady's day to die, because it surely was in my grandmother's ability to kill her.

My grandmother always talked about Jesus, but I never remember a day that she went to church. She did religiously believe in her dream book, though. How could a blind woman read a dream book without brail? Easily…through her five-year-old granddaughter: me! I learned to read with understanding at five years old by reading a psychic dream book.

Chapter 5
UPTOWN

I had to grow up fast, because there were things my grand-mother and my neighborhood required of me. Yes, there were other adults around, but somehow it always seemed like it was just "Momma"(Ms. Ella Mae) and me. We never called my real mother "Momma"; we just called her by her name, because my grandmother was "Momma."

My grandfather, likewise, was truly my daddy. My two sisters and I each had a different natural father, and none of them was around. Of our three fathers, mine was seen the most, because he had various businesses, legal and illegal, around the corner. He was into the numbers game. My grandmother ran the bolida, which is an illegal version of lotto. She often sent me to Ms. Tibby's house to deliver numbers and money. My grandmother and Ms. Tibby had a lot in common. They drank the small coca colas, frequently took BC and Stanback powders for headaches, and had respect on the streets.

My natural father was a highly respected man in the black community. He was a very handsome man, and was known for having nice-looking women. My father had the power to make you love him or hate him. He was not a man who joked around a lot, and he did not take orders easily from anybody. My father was the leader of a group called the "Boomerang Gang," which was famous for having burned down much of Jacksonville's downtown area in a race riot.

For the first 13 years of my life, my father never publicly claimed me as his daughter. But if you looked at my pecan-tan skin color and extremely curly hair (just like his), you would know I was Percy's daughter.

My father got my mother pregnant while he was still married to a beautiful, fair-skinned woman named Cleo. Cleo and my dad often had public fights, and she was a very outspoken woman. No matter what, Percy would never confess to her that he was the father of Ms. Ella Mae's granddaughter. As influential as my father was, whenever Ms. Ella Mae called, he would come running.

My Aunt Lillie Mae would tell the story of how my blind grandmother had vowed that if she found out my mother was pregnant from Percy, she would kill him. If some people would make such a threat, you might think they are just bluffing. However, from a person like my grandmother, no one would take it lightly.

Lillie Mae said that my grandmother waited on the porch for them to bring me home from the hospital. Her first words were, "What color is her skin?" and "What kind of hair does she have?" My grandmother never pursued my daddy, but he would bring her money periodically. For a while his wife did not know Percy's secret, but everybody on the streets knew I was Percy's daughter.

My dad eventually married a new wife, named Lolita. She was a fancy-dressing woman who wore her hair very high on her head. My dad's first wife left him with three children, two boys and a girl. I will never forget my sixth birthday party. All three of my dad's other children came, and I felt like I was on top of the world. My sister, Shawna, was the prettiest sight I'd ever seen. She had long, wavy black hair, and even though I had two sisters living with me at my grandmother's, I looked up to Shawna because she lived with my real daddy. I would have given anything to trade places with her.

Elliot was the youngest brother, and he was the one who spent the most time with me. He was very funny, and even as a very young man, he had a lot of girlfriends. The middle son was more laid back and played more of a big-brother role in my life. He would send me home from the bar before dark. I did not appreciate that very much, because when I was at my daddy's bar, I felt at home.

The Bar Scene

As a young girl I was drawn to the bar scene and loved the atmosphere there. Elliot was the exact opposite of my brother Rodney, who was always causing me to get in some kind of trouble. My father's bar was a block from my house, and every moment there was a thrill. They had "sissy shows" several times a week. These shows consisted of men impersonating famous female singers. The most fascinating thing was that after the show was over, they still lived liked women.

The apartment I lived in was one floor above a house full of homosexuals and transvestites. I have never contemplated nor been involved in a homosexual relationship, yet I was fascinated and drawn to men who lived that lifestyle. I loved the "sissies." I believe that this exposure enhanced the call of God on my life to minister to homosexuals. I spent a lot of time with them and saw them as "regular people." After being saved, I realized they are people with a problem...a problem that Jesus died for.

Uptown was a tough place. Either you "beat up" or you "*got* beat up." You had to earn a reputation on the streets in order to avoid constant harassment. Big Momma did not play around when it came to fighting. When confronted, our in-structions were not to come home until we kicked the life out of someone. Big Momma also told us that if one of us fought, *all* of us had to fight. So if one got dirty in a scuffle, we all rolled in the dirt in order to pass the test when we got home.

My grandmother never laid eyes on me in the natural, but despite her rough exterior I somehow knew that deep down inside, she loved me. Affection was rarely shown in our home and the words "I love you" were literally extinct. We all knew that we loved each other; we just did not know how to say it.

A child who grows without hearing those words will miss something in life. Those who never hear "I love you" will struggle later in life when someone tries to love them. They will have barriers around them, because they won't have the faith to believe in love. The Bible says that "faith comes by hearing," and it is difficult to receive true love as an adult when you have never heard of it as a child.

Thank God for Granddaddy

The closest bond we experienced as children was with our grandaddy, Mr. Bubba. I loved my grandaddy so much. He was the one who hugged us and spent time with us. He called us a nickname I will never forget: "Pooka - Packa - Pookas." It may sound silly, but it meant so much to hear those words. They were especially for us. To me, my grandfather was a mother and father in one package.

Every Friday was payday, and when grandaddy stepped off the city bus it was always with a big box of goodies. The one treat I particularly remember is Cracker Jacks. If anybody could put a smile on my face, it was my grandaddy, Mr. Bubba. When everybody was working, partying, fussing or just too busy, he always spent time with his granddaughters. He cooked dinner every night after he came home from work.

Grandaddy was an alcoholic for many years, but he would not sip a drink until he was sure we were bathed, fed and ready for bed. He drank Fleischmann's Gin with no chaser. A fifth would last him a night. He would drink and smoke his Camel cigarettes until he passed out, and we would laugh and play tricks on him when he had reached his limit.

I can still picture grandfather, sitting in a chair, nodding like a heroine addict with mucus running from his nose. We would hide under the bed or in the closet and yell to scare him. He would curse us out and try to run after us. But he rarely spanked us, and even if he did, we laughed while he tried to do it. Although people might say we had a very dysfunctional family situation, I am grateful for the ways my granddaddy made our house something of a home.

A Break-in Gone Bad

I will never forget the time a man broke into my aunt's window in the back of the house and put a knife to her neck to rape her. My mother was bathing my two sisters and me as we sang a song she had taught us. My mom was on the go a lot, so this moment when we sang together really sticks out in my mind. But our joy was interrupted by a terrible scream: "Momma, there is a man in the house!"

The house had a long, narrow hall, and my grandmother sat on the side of the entrance, where she would fall asleep. As the man frantically ran through the hall, he came past my grandmother. As I mentioned earlier, my grandmother always kept a switchblade in her bra. Though she was blind, her senses were keen. Timing the steps of the running assailant, with one hand she grabbed his shirt as he passed by, and with the other hand she commenced stabbing him.

Blood splattered everywhere. I looked around the corner of the room I was in, facing the entire scene. My grandmother was literally growling and cursing this man as she stabbed him over and over again. She had a death grip on him that he could not get loosed from.

As I looked into my grandmother's face, it appeared that she enjoyed every moment of what she was doing. As for the man, he looked as if he was about to go into shock. When he finally broke away, he tore the front screen from our door as he was getting out of the house. He had crept into the wrong window that night.

Of course, when you are uptown, anything can happen.

Chapter 6
SUCCESS!

One day I noticed my mom and my aunt bringing new furniture into the house. They said it was for "the new house." New house? This was dramatic news to us. Where would we move? Who would be our friends? My mother said we were moving to the woods. And it really happened.

We moved into a brand-new house in Sherwood Forest on the north side of town. The most shocking thing was that most of our neighbors were white. The closest I had ever been to white people was when we went shopping downtown. This was a culture shock! We even attended an integrated school, where white students sat next to me in classes.

All I ever knew about white people was that they either treated black people badly, beat them up, or used them to clean their houses like my Aunt Lillie Mae did. Eventually we got used to it, but the white people never did. Soon they all moved out of the neighborhood and everybody around us was black again. Nevertheless, we were bused to white schools.

By this time, my sisters and I were recognized as having extraordinary athletic ability. And my middle sister, Joy, and I were exceptionally bright and were put in advanced courses. The junior high school I attended had race riots all the time. Of course, I was on the front lines, inciting and initiating trouble.

I will never forget when a large group of us jumped a white boy who had thrown a brick at our bus. I was the first one on him. I pulled his hair from his head by the roots. In a rage, I cursed and kicked and beat up this white boy. I had no sense of guilt about this all, but actually found it rather enjoyable. The only thing that got me off of him was when I looked at the handful of his hair in my hand. It was full of bugs, and I was always afraid of bugs! I ran off wishing I could have gotten one more lick.

Familiar Spirits

My grandmother died when I was eight years old, but somehow it seemed as if she was still around. The same bad spirits that were on her were on me. I cursed fluently and could do so to the point of making someone cry. When Big Momma died, I didn't cry. I was sad for my mother and the rest of the family, and I'm sure I loved her deep down inside. But it was a relief to not have to be her eyes and hands anymore.

I had walked so close to grandmother that I found myself acting just like her. Fighting was like eating breakfast to me. If I did not have a fight at least once a week, I felt like something was missing in my life. Because of this, I started a gang with a group of the toughest girls in school. Everybody in the group had a day to fight somebody. If the person whose day it was to fight could not find an innocent bystander to jump on, we jumped on them!

I had moved from uptown, but uptown was still in me. Every time I had a confrontation with someone, I would hear my grandmother say, "Never let them hit you first. Always strike first and ask questions later!" This was the law that I lived by, because most of the people from uptown moved to Sherwood Forest and the cycle started all over again. I was the type that was at the root of all confusion in my school, but I never got caught. Despite all the masterminding and dirty tricks I did, I was only suspended twice from school, once in junior high and once in high school.

I maintained honor roll status and won every essay contest I entered. I could always express myself creatively in black and white, and I was not too bad verbally. I did have a Southern accent that stood out in certain environments, but it never bothered me, because I was confident in who I was.

I was a terror to my enemies but a friend to whoever I was a friend to. I never believed in backstabbing true friends, and dedication to friends has always been a highlight of my life. Because of my athletic ability, I was very popular with the younger students.

Breaking the Molds

The junior high school I attended had never had a black student as president of the Student Council or homecoming queen. I did not like the fact that blacks were never voted into these positions, and decided to do something about it: I entered my name on the ballot. Most blacks, however, did not pursue these positions, because they were brain-locked on the fact that no one of color had ever won before.

I always knew I was born to make a difference. I was sure that if what I was doing did not fit into the mold of things, I could break the old mold and fashion a new one. The key words to describe me were catalyst, initiator and instigator. If I felt strongly enough about something, I knew it could happen. I did not yet have the slightest idea of who Jesus was, but as I look back on my early tendencies I can easily see why God chose me: He knew I would not stop until the job was done!

When I decided to run for office in my junior high school, I calculated that the school had 70% white students and 30% black students. I knew I could get white votes from the 7th and 8th grade fans that liked me because I played sports. I also was confident that there were so many pretty little white girls waiting to ride on that homecoming float that by the time they split their votes ten ways, I was destined to win. My only test was to rally the blacks and get the black girls not to run, so the votes would not split.

My strategy worked. Only one other black girl entered the contest, and she was not popular enough to make a difference. I became the first black homecoming queen at Highlands Junior High School in Jacksonville, Florida. The momentum from this accomplishment was like a domino effect, and I was also voted president of a 95% white student council.

After winning these contests, I found that the titles meant nothing to me. I could care less about school politics, and all I wanted was my picture in the yearbook as homecoming queen. I pulled the fire alarms a few months after that, and both titles were taken from me. The only thing that hurt me during incident was being removed from the softball team, because I was one of two blacks who made the team and started. This crushed my heart. It was one of the most remorseful times in my life. I was not sorry for what I did, but just sorry I got caught. They took the titles, but they could never take away the fact that I succeeded in breaking the mold.

I graduated from Highlands and went to Jean Ribault Senior High School, home of the Trojans. When we said "Ribault," we did it with pride. I was truly proud to wear the baby blue, black and white, and I excelled in both athletics and academics.

However, the dean of girls was constantly on my trail. She was a black middle-aged woman with a strong personality. I was not afraid of her, but I realized she had the power to make or break me academically or athletically. She knew I was a getting into mischief, but she could never catch me, since few people would volunteer information.

My home life did not entail much supervision, and my mother had no control over my life by this time. I went to school when I wanted to, came home as late as I wanted, and smoked cigarettes in my mother's face. This is something that always puzzled me: Why would an athlete of my caliber smoke? It was strange and, as I later learned, demonic.

Running for Office Again

Many of my senior classmates hated my guts, but they put up with me long enough to get me out of their face. Behind closed doors they talked about me, but because of my reputation as a vicious fighter, very few would confront me directly. Although I knew I had some enemies, I got a crazy idea: running for homecoming queen and Student Council president at Jean Ribault Senior High.

I would not have attempted it if it were not for the challenge. Though Ribault was 99% black (we had a few white kids in Special Education Classes), it was nevertheless divided into sociological groups. There were well-off students from nice neighborhoods, streetwise students, stuck-up students, athletes, honor roll students and administration pets.

I really did not fit into any of these groups. Even most of the streetwise students were not on my level, because I spent all my extra time "uptown," which was another level. I played sports, but didn't fit into the "jock" group either. After competitions, when all the other athletes went to neighborhood parties, I ran "uptown" to see the "sissy show" and watch people get beat up until they were unconscious. Even though I was *in* high school, I was not *of* it, because all of my best friends were eight to 20 years older than I was. So for somebody like me, who wasn't a part of the system, to win these prestigious titles was a seemingly impossible challenge. Yet I was never one to run from challenges.

Just as in junior high, I needed a strategy. Ribault had a few hundred junior and senior class students, but close to a thousand freshmen. That was my answer: work on the freshmen. While everybody solicited the vote of the popular students, I went to the unpopular freshmen who nobody paid any attention to, and made them feel very special. As in junior high, I won homecoming queen and Student Council president with a clean sweep.

I will never forget when the dean of girls heard I was running for these positions, and called me into her office. Laughing in my face, she said, "If you think for one minute I will sign the paper for you to run, you are dead wrong."

I ran crying to the principal of the school, and he comforted me immediately. As I looked into his eyes, I began to feel very uncomfortable. He walked over to me, grabbed the back of my head and kissed me. I could not believe it. He was such an old man in my eyes, and I felt very violated. He looked at me and said, "Don't you worry about a thing. You can run for whatever your heart desires." I ran out of his office, never to tell a soul.

After this experience, the dean of girls immediately called me into her office and signed my paper, with no questions asked. The principal's help did not cause me to win, but without his influence, I could never have been on the ballot.

For the first time in my life, I saw that on the road to success you will be expected to go through "tollbooths" every now and then. Despite this, I was not willing to play the game. Often the tollbooths are at the entrance to some new level, whether in God or the devil. There is a price that must be paid either way, but the key factor is to know whose gates are you traveling through.

Chapter 7
INTRODUCTION
TO WITCHCRAFT

My mother married a man who was seven years older than me, and we moved from Sherwood Forest to an area called Forest Hills. This neighborhood was a little slower streetwise, but on a gradual decline as far as crime and the other things that came along with it.

Because my new step father was not much older than me, we got along like cats and dogs. Many times our confrontations became physical. I can remember crying, chest to chest, with this 250-pound, 6'4" military man. I got my hands on a pistol and kept it under my bed, vowing to kill him if he pushed me too far. He despised me, and my feelings were no better for him.

In retrospect, I can see what he was up against. He came into a ready-made environment and tried to tame a wild animal— me. At the age of 14 I was staying out to 6 a.m., falling into the doorway deliriously drunk. I never particularly liked alcohol, but during this time in my life I turned to it as a result of peer pressure.

I was very close to a set of twins who lived down the street from me. They were grown women, yet we had much in common. Everywhere Carmen and Carla went, I was in their shadow. In clubs and on every set, we become the party triplets. There were times when we would go to the club on Friday night and not come home until Sunday. Although Carla showed some restraint in her rowdiness, Carmen and I took chances to the limit.

A Perilous Date

There were two young men who consistently called us about going on a blind date. As usual, Carla declined the invitation. Carmen and I got dressed up and left with these guys without any money. They pulled out marijuana and we smoked until I practically felt blind. I was having difficulty keeping my eyes open, when all of a sudden a ruckus broke out in the back seat. I was so high on drugs that it all seemed like a dream.

The guy in the back seat was choking Carmen, and she was cursing and fighting him with all her strength. Though we hung out a lot with seedy characters, we were not into sleeping around. Hard as it may be to believe, both of us were virgins. We just liked to party.

What my ears then heard took the breath from my body. The driver said, "Hey man, do you want to take these two where we took the last two?" Despite the numbing effect of the drugs, I was gripped by an unbearable fear and the merciless taunt of the demons that accompanied the marijuana.

I looked at the driver and told him I was only 14 years old. I tried to hide under the cover of immaturity, but he did not fall for it. He responded with a sarcastic remark, "You were old enough to get in my car and smoke a reefer, so you're old enough to give me what I want!"

Outside of my own neighborhood, I was not very familiar with Jacksonville but I noticed they were driving us in circles. They tried to convince us to have consensual sex with them, but we never did. Then they gave us an ultimatum. Have sex or walk! They dropped us off close to a National Guard Armory, where a dance was going on. We knew the band that was playing, and we went in and partied like nothing ever happened! But I never went on a blind date again.

The twins and I were known as "groupies." We hung around where the popular local bands played, and that's what I lived for. My weekly goal was simply to get a new outfit, have some spending change for a few sodas, and money to get in the club. I was still in high school, so this meant living a double life. I had fake identification that said I was 18, and my body said I was every bit of 21. I still participated in sports somehow and in the heat of the season would slack up on my nightlife.

Mother's New Friends

My mother and I had little to do with each other. She was living her life and I was living mine. Her new friends were very strange. As they sat in the living room on a Wednesday night at 10:30, I would be walking out the door and they would question my mom about where I was going at that time of night. I told them it was none of their business, and my mother asked them to leave me alone.

I often heard my mother's new friends tell her there was something "special" about me. They said I was the one they had to watch out for. It turned out that these new associates of my mother were nothing less than modern-day witches.

One thing I've learned since coming on the Lord's side is that the spirits of mammon, religion and divination walk hand in hand. In Acts 16:16 a woman with a fortune-telling spirit was following the apostles around. She is a prime example of what I call "three evils in one":

> 1. **Divination** - This comes from the root word "divine," which means to operate in a power inspired by a supreme or supernatural spiritual force; to control.

> 2. **Religion** - This spirit hides under the guise of a form

of godliness and repetition. The woman with the fortune-telling spirit only mimicked what she heard.

3. Mammon - The Bible states that the woman had a spirit of divination, which comes from the Greek word *python*, and she was a soothsayer for gain.

The church is often infiltrated by people who are under the control of these spirits. They pretend to draw others to Jesus, but are doing so by a pseudo (false) or substitute power. Most of the time they claim some special title for themselves, such as Mother, Father, Pastor, Prophet, Evangelist or Apostle. These deceivers are much more dangerous than the TV psychics or the palm readers on the highway, who at least are honest about who they are: witches, warlocks and voodoo doctors.

My exposure as a young girl to these occultic friends of my mother planted a seed in me. I began to hate witchcraft with a passion. In my present ministry, God has given me a burden and an assignment to confront the witches with the truth. It is the truth that will make them free.

Hannah and the Dog Races

One particular lady who was regularly at my house was always at odds with me, and we could never agree on anything. Her name was Hannah, and she was the one that always said I was "special." She had a big house a few blocks from ours. Even in the daytime, she burned candles all over her house.

Hannah's house was always filthy, and my mom sent us over to help her clean it. It was so junky that there was no way we could make it look much better. After we cleaned for hours, instead of paying us money, she fed us. If I knew what I know now, I would have never eaten from that table. The food looked strange, and the portions were very small. I urged my sisters to leave that house and never return again.

Something made me hate to even hear the name "Hannah." She used occult powers to give people numbers to gamble with, and her followers considered her to be a spiritual "bishop." She had churches in several cities, yet she did not attend church herself.

Once I saw Hannah tie rags around a broom with a flammable liquid on it. She put a match to it and ran it up and down my mother's back. The skin did not burn, but it turned a sooty black. I do not remember if this was a dream or vision, or if I really saw it. However, when I asked my mother about it, she said it was true.

My mother also said that Hannah and some other women tried to cast demons out of her. They put her in a bathtub and poured ammonia on her. Ammonia is one of the tools witches use. They also use such things as red strings, crosses, salt and sulfur. Ammonia is supposed to keep evil spirits away.

One Christmas season my mom and these women struck it rich at the dog races. They took hundred-dollar bills and laid them in a liquid that appeared to be water. The money was supposed to multiply. Instead of multiplying, the money actually decreased—because I took out $300 for my Christmas money and went shopping! After stealing the wet money, I quickly caught the bus to the mall. I smiled as I proudly wore my new coat and boots, and everybody else involved was soon broke again.

I hated the dog races with a passion. The dogs at the racetrack lived and ate better that I did. We lost two homes to gambling, and fortunately that was a demon I never entertained.

Unmasking the Devil's Tactics

I eventually got so rebellious that my mother sought help in putting me under some kind of control. She did not know that rebellion was as the spirit of witchcraft. Hannah suggested that my mother needed to take me "to see someone." When I got in the car, I had no idea who I was going to see. My mother dropped me off and left me in a back room with a slanted roof, with a big black man. The room had one table, with a lamp without a shade and two chairs.

The man began to tell me things about myself that no one else knew. He tried to give me a small bottle of oil, and said if I bathed in it, I would be the fastest sprinter in the world. I am so glad I never took his offer. The devil was trying to buy my soul in exchange for fame.

I was so rebellious that I rebelled against satan himself! I told him what he could do with his oil, but the devil did not take too kindly to my refusal of his offer. Things really got rough after that. I did not turn satan down so I could follow Jesus. I was merely trying to be my own god, and I worshiped the "god of self." Even though I did not believe in witchcraft, I was still being affected by it.

Since being saved, I have understood witchcraft in a very clear way. God's people are truly destroyed by what they do not know (Hos. 4:6). Most believers think that as long as they learn about Jesus, the devil can't harm them. But God gave us both offensive and defensive weapons against the enemy. My present knowledge about the dark side was gained through a process of growth and experience. If I had pretended that the demonic obstacles I faced were not there, I am sure I would have died an early death.

Knowing the devices and tactics of the enemy gives us a strong defense. Any army without good secret intelligence agents will not be successful. I am a traitor from the other side. I walked out on the devil years ago. I no longer work for him, and I found out that God has better benefits for his employees. The devil wanted to give me a term life policy, but God gave me eternal life. I would not trade in my "whole life" policy with Jesus for anything in the world.

It is still hard for me to believe that people willingly serve the devil. My mother wanted the benefits of hanging out with practitioners of witchcraft, but she never truly wanted to give her soul to satan. She did not understand it was a package deal. When she realized who she was really dealing with, she walked out on her longtime buddies.

My mother told me about a time when she went to Hannah's house unexpectedly on her lunch break. Hannah's house was full bloom with candles as usual, but this time she had her altar to satan fixed up very boldly. The door of Hannah's room was cracked open, and when my mother peeped in, Hannah was naked, rubbing something on the floor. On her altar were a black cloth and statues of Mary holding the baby Jesus. When my mother asked her what she was doing, she said she was "getting niggers off of her!"

Hannah's response was in a deep voice that was not her own. The demons that spoke through this woman told my mother that she was the main person they needed, promising that they would give her power like Jim Jones (another devil worshiper who came in the name of Jesus). Hannah adored Jim Jones and often spoke of how wonderful he was.

I have not seen Hannah since I met Jesus, but I trust that the day will come when I can look her directly in her eyes and tell her that Jesus is Lord...join Him or die! Exodus 22:18 says,

"Thou shall not suffer a witch to live." The word "suffer" in the Hebrew is *nathan*, and it means to lift up, recompense, grant, ordain, render or send out. The word "witch" is *kashaph* in Hebrew and means to whisper a spell, to enchant or control the minds of people, or to operate in any power that is not Holy Spirit initiated and controlled.

Mixing Witchcraft and Religion

The key aspect of witchcraft is control. That is why rebellion is related to witchcraft. To rebel is "to work against or oppose by force (power)." Any time a true move of the Holy Spirit is opposed, witchcraft is at hand. Controlling spirits often work against the servants and the work of God. While their immediate target may be the vessel, in actuality, they oppose God. Whenever a person can control or maneuver their gifts as they please, it is witchcraft.

The Holy Spirit is not a switch that we turn on and cut off. Everything we do in the name of Jesus should be "as the Spirit wills." It is the will of man that makes many people cross the line and find themselves on the other side. This is how the satanic counterfeit creeps into the church.

I have a half sister who I've occasionally associated with since I have been in Jesus. I found out that she was operating in witchcraft, but I didn't know if she was deeply involved or not. The Holy Spirit impressed me to call and confront her. I specifically asked if she knew she was working witchcraft. She admitted that she did. I then asked her if she knew she was serving the devil and that she and I served two different gods. Again, she said she did. Because she operated in a spirit that opposed God, I had no communication with her for many years. However, she is now saved and is wholeheartedly serving God.

The word "live" in the Exodus 22:18 passage about handling witches is *chayah,* which means to preserve or to say to be whole in the existing state. To preserve means to help maintain, cover or protect. I cannot cover up or cloak evil. One of the responsibilities of a priest is to teach people the difference between the holy and the unholy, and between clean and unclean (Lev. 10:10). This is a responsibility that is often neglected by church leaders today.

The first person I ever knew who called herself an evangelist was the mother of one of my best friends, named Helen. She was a very pretty young girl with long, wavy hair. Helen and I and a young lady named Cheryl were best friends. We all had long, pretty hair, but Helen was light-skinned, I was brown-skinned and Cheryl was dark. We hung out together so much that everyone thought we were sisters.

Jealous because Helen was so pretty, Helen's mom beat her and treated her differently from the rest of her children. Helen had to clean for hours just to get her mom's permission to leave the house. She also had many little brothers who she was required to take care of. I watched her mother put on a flowered hat and drive off to church in her station wagon every Sunday. I also saw her mom curse a relative and then rejoice when he broke his back. Upon hearing of the relative's accident, she ran around the house, yelling, "I know my stuff works!"

Today two of Helen's little brothers are on death row for murder, one is a homosexual, and the other had a life sentence for murder but was released for turning state evidence against the other two brothers. Yeah, I guess her mom's stuff does really work!

The ladies my mother used to associate with still operate in witchcraft. One of them tried to come to Jesus, but because of the spiritual connection that was broken, she was literally tormented to death. Even though she died a torturous death, I believe she sincerely came to Christ before she died, and is now resting in the presence of the Lord.

The name of this lady who converted out of witchcraft was Ms. Ruby. She was a small black woman who operated fluently in "roots," which is a common term for witchcraft in the Black community. She announced to the others in the witchcraft group that she had chosen Jesus, and asked them to forgive her if she had trespassed against them in anyway. One lady named Tessa refused to forgive her, and hated her immensely. My mother heard the woman say that before the sun went down, Ms. Ruby would pay.

Ms. Ruby started dying so quickly that the doctors could not keep up with all her ailments. Her organs all began to fail. When people have afflictions that are rooted in witchcraft, medical science cannot determine the source. You cannot solve a spiritual problem with a natural answer. As I often tell people, "If you've got a devil problem, you need a Jesus answer!"

Chapter 8
UNFAMILIAR TERRITORY

Before I graduated from high school, I met a young man who asked me to live with him and have his baby. He was older than I was and had many girl friends. But I needed a change in environment, so I accepted his offer. I really cared for him, and he took good care of our baby, Mike-Mike.

I graduated from high school pregnant. Again, I had to resign from my homecoming queen and Student Council positions. I still had the consolation of winning, and my pictures were already in the yearbook. During my senior year, I went to school for three quarters and obtained a 4.0 GPA. Because I knew my grades were already good enough to graduate, I didn't bother showing up for my last term at all. My 4.0 turned into a C average. I just wanted to graduate.

My senior year at Ribault lacked the prom, grad-night and other special activities that a normal 17-year-old would give anything for. I had to force myself to walk down the aisle to receive my diploma—six months' pregnant. And I bought a yearbook, because the memories meant a lot.

I lived such a fast life in high school that I never competed athletically with my full potential. And in accepting the offer to have my boyfriend's baby, I lost the opportunity to obtain a track scholarship. My baby's father was very successful in his career and an excellent provider, but something was still missing. Hesitantly, I followed him to Portland, Oregon, on a job transfer. All I had was my son, my clothes, and an approved financial aid packet for college.

Oregon was the cleanest place I had ever seen. As a matter of fact, it was too clean. There was no ghetto, no uptown, and no sissies. I did not think I would make it there. I had a perfect little family, except I was only married by common law. All I had to do was say the word, and my boyfriend would have been happy to have everything legalized, but something in me said "no."

Something Is Missing!

My baby's father had become a parental figure to me. He handled everything. My life consisted of taking care of the house and putting things on layaway at the mall for him to get out.

Something was still missing! I convinced him that if I did not do something with my life, I was going back to Florida. He took me to the community college in Mount Hood, Oregon. I had never seen mountains before. As I looked down the street, the mountains looked like a picture book. All I could think about was how my street friends would trip on this scenery.

The first office I sought at Mt. Hood Community College was the track office. I walked into the office of the head track coach and introduced myself. I had no idea that this man had connections with the Olympic Advisory Board. I told him that I was enrolling in his school and would run on his track team with the following conditions. I would pay for my schooling one quarter, but I wanted a full scholarship when the winter term came. I promised him I would outrun every woman on his team.

In a few weeks I broke every school sprint record for women. I was running with a speed I had never known before, and soon I qualified for the nationals. My coach was a very influential man, and he pulled strings to get me in a popular televised meet. My event was the 60-meter indoors, and it was like a grand finale of the night.

My baby's father had never seen me run. He managed a concession company in the coliseum and stood in the corridor on his break to watch the race. They turned the lights out and put a spotlight on every competitor, going down their list of accomplishments and titles in track and field. When they came to me, the commentator merely said, "In this lane, we have Kim Parrish." I was nobody on the track and field circuit but I had a determination in my heart to be a winner.

The gun went off. In a matter of seconds, I blew the entire field off the track. Everybody was wondering where I came from. I believe this was the night when my baby's father realized I would not be with him forever.

Faster and Faster

Every time I stepped on the track, my legs moved faster, my head got bigger and my temper ran hotter. I was one of two blacks on the team, and there were only 20 blacks in the entire college. The assistant track coach was black and a real "brother." He made me feel comfortable on the team, even though my dialect clearly separated me from my teammates.

Even the other blacks in the college were a lot different from me. They acted more "white" in their speech and mannerisms, and they would often giggle at the way I talked. My ghetto/country accent also made it very embarrassing for me to ask questions in class. Despite this, I refused to change just so I could be like everybody else. I could have tried to talk like everyone else, but I took pride in who I was.

At the end of the first semester, I had a 3.65 GPA with a

16-hour study workload, an 18-month-old baby, housework, a part-time job, track practice and travel. I was determined to be all I could be, but I depended solely on "self." My coach would take me to local Kiwanis meetings to introduce me to people who donated money to the college. These meetings were at 6 a.m., once a week.

I tried to ignore my coach's knocking on my apartment door at 5 a.m., and usually would not be dressed. I would do anything to miss what I call his "Ku Klux Klan" meetings. I was the only black face in the dark of early morning, and I wondered if one of his lodge members would have a flashback and feel like having an old-fashioned lynching! Although I would have preferred sleeping in, my coach was persistent and I ended up attending the meeting regularly. Although I got special treatment on the team because of the level I was running on, it wasn't an easy transition for a black from "uptown."

Surviving Culture Shock

Not only my college, but everything about Oregon was a culture shock for me. It didn't take me long to discover that I needed someone to mail grits from Florida. What kind of city doesn't sell grits? I became very homesick. Oregon had a black radio station called "KABU" that aired one hour on Sunday. That was my highlight of the week, but on the other 167 hours, I became a hardcore rock music fan.

Once when I was traveling with the team, we stopped in the mountains on an Indian Reservation. Because of the intense hatred for blacks in that area, everyone seriously advised me not to get off the bus. Even though I was raised "uptown," I was not a fool. I stayed low on the bus and asked them to please hurry back with my food. What kind of place was this that a track star could not eat in a restaurant with the rest of the team? Home was looking better every day.

I qualified for nationals in four events. My times had only been beaten by one young lady, who was from Nebraska. One day after track practice, a female runner sat in the whirlpool with me. She was full-blooded Cherokee and a pretty good athlete. When I pulled my leg out of the ice, it was purple. She yelled, "Look at your leg, you're really a nigger there!" The athletes on my team thought it was perfectly normal to call me a nigger. Yet I would hear them telling each other, "Whatever you do, don't call Kim a nigger—she doesn't like that!"

I tried to correct my teammates through threats and physical abuse. Many times I found myself cursing like my grandmother did, and those in my college swore they had never heard such vulgar things. Several times I collared teammates in the shower room, promising to break their legs after nationals. From the coaches on down, I was increasingly regarded as a crazy person.

Hollow Victories

Junior College Nationals were held in San Angelo, Texas, where it was 105 degrees in the shade. Most of my teammates could not handle the humidity, but I was right at home. As our bus transported us from the airport and we approached the campus where the meet was being held, my eyes lit up with excitement. Black people were everywhere! I felt like kissing the ground. One of my teammates yelled, "Gollee, would ya look at the niggers!" By this time, I was tired of fighting, and understood their ignorance. In my mind I said, "I'm gonna be the fastest nigger in the nation!"

It seemed that every time I hit the track, I broke a record. The newspapers interviewed the young lady from Nebraska and asked her what she thought about me and the way I was running. She confidently stated that I would burn myself out by the final, and she would win the gold. Nobody interviewed me, but I knew those gold medals had my name on them. I did not burn out easily.

I won first place in three races, beating the Nebraska sprinter and anyone else who stepped on the track. It was my season. It seemed like I could not lose. At the end of the day, my coach announced that I was anchoring the 4x400 relay, but I really didn't want to. I was already in shock from winning the 4x100 relay with three white girls running the first three legs. This was unheard of! Everybody knows white girls can't sprint. They were the only white girls on the track, and everybody else was black as night. But to my surprise, they passed me the baton in first place. Three white girls and one black won the National Junior College 4x100 meter relay, and I could not take all the glory.

Yet now my coach was trying to take the same four and win the 4x400? Lightning cannot strike twice in the same place! But it did. I was given the award for the Most Outstanding Female Athlete in the Nation. After calling home to let everyone know what had taken place, I forgave the white girls who had called me nigger all season. That meant I had nothing to look forward to, not even a good fight.

I went back to my room and cried after all that great victory, because I still felt a void in my life. *There must be more to life than this!* I kept saying to myself. I know for a fact that the superstars you see in the sports and entertainment industry are not as happy as you might think. Life without Jesus is miserable to everybody!

National Championships

My coach talked me into running in the U.S. National Championships. The good part was that I got to go home to Florida to train for a month before competition. At least I thought it was good. The Bible says there is a way that seems right to a man, but the end of it is death. That summer I packed my bags, grabbed my baby, and went back to Florida. I took as much as I could carry on the plane, and all the time I knew I would never return to Oregon. All I could see ahead of me were open doors, but I had no idea I was headed for a dead end.

Training did not go well in Florida. Trying to live a double life again distracted me. I tried to fit the club, uptown and the sissy show into my training schedule. I even got to experience the desire of my heart…to live with my natural father. He had another girlfriend, named Ruth, and she had a daughter from him named Connie. For the first time in my life, I felt like Percy's daughter. A newspaper article came out about my track accomplishments, and it recognized me as Percy's daughter.

My father's first wife found out I was really his child when I was 13 years old. By this time, she had divorced him and remarried. I was trying to find my sister and two brothers, and someone told me they lived on the boat dock. To my surprise, my father's ex-wife opened the door and said, "Come in baby, I know you are Percy's daughter. You look just like my youngest son." Even at this time, she called my dad all kinds of names, but she could not deny the resemblance between us.

My father drove me to Orlando, and I flew out to Sacramento, California, for the American Team Nationals. During the month I was home for training, I had received scholarship offers from almost every state in the nation. I could have gone anywhere, but wanted to be a part of the best sprint team in the nation, which at the time was Florida State. Yet when I pursued going there, Florida State was the only college that did not show interest in me.

Big names and bright lights brought distraction to the

effectiveness of my race at the Nationals. I ran poor times, worse than I had run all season. As I look back, I see this as a great lesson for ministers of the gospel of Jesus Christ. We will find ourselves faced with the similar peer pressures, and our souls will be blinded from our true calling by the demon of pseudo-success.

A New Man

Chandra Cheeseborough was a three-time Olympian and my teammate in high school. She introduced me to all the big-name runners, but there was one I would never forget. Marcus Riley was a world-class 200m champion, and fit well into my goal of snatching up a famous athlete. I had already cut ties with my baby's father, and I immediately flipped over Marcus. He appeared to do the same over me.

The head track coach for Florida State University was in line ahead of me at the airport, and he was with the coach from the University of Florida. The coach from the University of Florida had been at Junior College Nationals, and told the Florida State coach what a sprinter I was. Although Florida State had shown no interest in me before, this brief episode turned everything around and opened the door for me to go there.

I went back home and spent the summer with my sissies and kept in contact with Marcus, long distance at my dad's expense.

In the fall semester I packed my bags and moved to Tallahassee. For the first time, my son was separated from me. His father begged me to leave him with his parents, which I knew was best for him until I was prepared to adequately support him.

Meanwhile, I moved in with Marcus, the sprint star. He was a very neat man. He was a model and bragged on himself all the time. He did not wear anything that was not name brand, and what people thought of him meant more than anything. Our relationship was awesome on a personal basis, and we were best friends.

The problem came from the public and his friends. I simply did not fit in the mold, and it was one I could not break. Marcus and I spent a lot of time together at the beginning of our relationship, but this slowly declined. Girls that had previous relationships with him would frequently come to the door crying, and he would treat them so badly. I felt sorry for them, but there was nothing I could do to help them…he was *my* man!

The reason Florida State could not promise me a scholarship was not because of my ability, but because of the availability of contracts. At the last minute, on the first day of school, a scholarship became available. I was used to living on the edge and going the long way around, so this was right down my alley.

Marcus started being late picking me up from classes. He also left me home by myself many nights, but I was content just sleeping in his bed. For the first time, marriage came to my mind, but it was not on his agenda. He was very jealous and never wanted me around other men. We began to have violent encounters, and I was exposed to all the other women he had besides me. I moved into my own apartment and soon found myself crying on the other side of Marcus' door, with someone else on the inside with him.

Chapter 9
THE CRAZY HOUSE

Marcus and I were like yo-yos to each other, and the violence got so bad that the coaches barred him from the track field. I would sneak off and meet him against the orders of my coaches. My track performance was going down the drain. I was running a half-second slower in the 100 meters, and my times were about the same as I ran in high school.

Eventually my track scholarship was taken away. I left the track team with two years of NCAA eligibility left. I vowed that one day I would return. Today as I write my story, my son Michael is the fastest quarter miler at Florida State University. He is tenths of a second from Olympic Trial qualifying time. I myself may not have returned, but God has allowed my offspring to go for me.

Being a regular student at Florida State University was easy to adapt to. I missed track and field, but as long as I stayed away from it, I was fine. I never watched it on television, because it caused a deep emptiness on the inside. One day my roommate and I played a trick on Marcus to make him think I was going to commit suicide. I emptied a bottle of pills and hid them under the bathroom counter. I told my roommate, but when he arrived, it seemed as if she forgot.

Marcus stuck his fingernails in my side and walked me to his car. Two weeks before that he had jumped on me like a dog on a cat for having a football player at my apartment. In retaliation, I had taken a knife and cut the top of his convertible into two pieces. It was clear that the brutality was getting worse.

After Marcus put me in the car, I was laughing all the way to the hospital, telling him we were playing a joke. Marcus wanted to prove to my coach that the confusion in our relationship was not one-sided. He called my coach and they talked me into signing papers for treatment of attempted suicide.

I never had any intentions of killing myself; I just wanted to get Marcus' attention. Out of respect for my track coach, I foolishly agreed to sign the papers. They gave me medicine to pump my stomach, but I had no idea of the pain I was about to encounter. With only a couple of pills in my stomach, the medicine made me throw up violently. But all I could do was dry heave, because nothing was there.

The doctor came in and said that anytime there was a threat of suicide, they had to keep the patient overnight. They took me by ambulance to another hospital. I didn't realize until it was too late that I was being committed to a crazy house. I could not believe it. The intake counselor looked as if he should have been a patient himself! I tried to tell him that it was all a mistake. He told me I would not be able to leave that place until he approved it.

I did not eat for three days. Other patients would take my food, and I let them have it. The weirdness of uptown was nothing compared to this. I was surrounded with people who were not in control of themselves. I knew I had to sleep at night, so I tried not to stir up anything or make enemies. There were murderers, anorexics and reprobates in this strange hospital. Where did I fit into this picture?

I called the one person I knew would help me: Mike-Mike's dad. He comforted me, but by the time I contacted him, the track coach had signed me out. This whole episode put a bad taste in my mouth for Marcus, and staying away from him got easier.

Back to the Streets

I moved from the Governor Square Mall area in Tallahassee to a highly concentrated drug area. I felt like I was home again. Something drew me to the streets. I was introduced to a place called French Town in the city. It was just like uptown.

I started dating a bus driver, and through him met a young man named Danny. Danny was a drug dealer, but he was the most handsome man I'd ever met. Danny lived with his girlfriend and had a baby boy. He was a lot older than I was, but he had many other female associates who would ride his bus route. We became partners.

Another friend introduced me to cocaine, but snorting it never did anything for me. One day my friend and I passed a young lady who looked like death. Her hair was messed up and she looked as if she weighed 50 pounds soaking wet. My friend called her a "rock star," but I could not even relate to what he was saying.

Danny came to my apartment to rest and make money. During this time in my life, everyone I met was in the dope scene. Marcus popped up a couple of times, but now my heart was geared toward Danny. Danny treated me as someone special. He would leave my house at 3:00 a.m. and go home to his girlfriend and son, but I would not linger on the thought. Deep down on the inside the fear of him leaving me was there, yet I refused to entertain it. The young lady he lived with constantly put pressure on him to marry her, but he and I kept getting closer.

Leslie, the mother of Danny's baby, was not streetwise, and he kept her out of his business. I was the one he did business with. Danny and I became lovers, best friends, and business partners. It was a relationship that someone could write an entire book about.

At a party one night, I met Henry, a man who was on the FBI's 10 Most Wanted List. Drug money comes easily and spends quickly, and Henry would order Red Lobster for the entire party. It was nothing for him to spend $2500 a night on food. He had a radio-security system that listened to all police transmissions, and he would get high and sit in front of the door with high-powered weapons, threatening to blow the police away if they tried anything.

I was one of many young girls who would hangout in the condominium. Henry would give three girls $12,000 and tell them to split it up and go shopping. But the drug-dealer mentality and lifestyle is not just about money and drugs. It is also about the power to control people's lives. I watched Henry treat people like dogs, and they willing submitted, just to get one hit of cocaine.

I learned later that the strongman of the spirit of addiction is *pharmakeia*. This Greek word means medication by magic. *Pharmakeia* is another word for sorcery or witchcraft, because it has a mood-altering or mind-controlling effect. God wants to be the one who controls our mind, and in order for it to be controlled, it must first be renewed. *Pharmakeia* works against the will of God in one's life, and therefore is equivalent to rebellion, which is as witchcraft.

Me? A Drug Trafficker?

One day I was at Henry's house and approached him with a question. I asked if he knew everybody who was in his house at the moment. Henry told me he didn't, for some were new visitors. Henry liked to be surrounded by people, because it gave him a sense of authority. No king can reign without a kingdom. What is a leader without people who follow?

Those who surrounded Henry thought he was so important,

not realizing that his insecure ego was actually fed by our presence and allegiance. One day I asked him how he knew one of his associates wasn't an undercover cop. Henry looked at me with a blank stare. I had his attention. After that conversation, Henry began to put his trust in me, and let me store garbage bags of dope at my house.

Eventually Henry was arrested and imprisoned, but we still kept in contact. He set up appointments for me to meet a Cuban man who was incarcerated in federal prison. I was put on this man's visitors list and saw him once a week. The purpose of the meetings was for him to instruct me on how to traffic cocaine without getting caught—which was pretty ironic since he had apparently been caught himself. It was not until the day before my first trip that I realized I had a new occupation: drug trafficker.

Nobody ever asked me if I wanted to participate in all this, they just assumed that I would do their bidding. One day Danny rented a car for me and told me to pick up a girl in Tampa with the same name as mine. This young lady knew the ropes of the drug trade, and went with me because it was my first time.

I was told to go to a phone booth on a particular corner in Miami. From that phone booth they directed me to three more. Later I learned that they were watching me to see if I was being followed. Three beautiful Cuban women picked me up and took me to a hotel and gave me empty suitcases. Even though I only had a restricted driver's license, I was driving to Miami to do a drug deal. I was really living on the edge.

The next day one of the women picked me up and took me to a place with more cocaine than I could ever imagine. I was in much too deep to turn around now. These Cubans owned a furniture store that was so exclusive you had to make an appointment to see their furniture. I had been trained well and given explicit instructions, and something told me I had better follow them.

The young lady offered to give me more cocaine than I was told to pick up, but I refused. The drug kingpin in prison had warned me never to take more than I was instructed to. Nevertheless, I left there with more cocaine than I had ever seen in my life. I had no idea that the young lady who traveled with me was an addict. She was a real "rock star." The term "rock" refers to the crack form of cocaine, once it is cooked in a test tube to its pure state. It is called "crack" because it cracks or makes a popping noise when you put fire to it in order to smoke it. So when you smoke crack they say you are "on that rock."

I do not want to get ahead of the story, but I must say I'm so glad that I am on the "Rock" that counts today. Jesus is my Rock, and there is no unrighteousness in Him. He is the Rock in which I hide myself and am not ashamed, for I am not ashamed of the gospel of Jesus Christ.

I was on my way back to Tallahassee, with plenty of drugs to put some "fire" on the streets—fuel for the hapless "rock stars" addicted to crack. Rock stars have no control of their lives. They can only affect the lives of others around them in a negative way. Crack addicts reproduce other crack addicts. If you hang around long enough, that controlling spirit will be released against you. There was a time when I would say what I would "never do." But I learned better than that, because whatever you plant seed into will eventually sprout up in your living room.

The young lady and I sniffed cocaine all the way to Tallahassee. Cocaine is not an opiate. Opiates induce sleepiness, but cocaine does the opposite, speeding things up. By the time I reached Tallahassee, I was zooming and paranoid about getting caught. I was so afraid that I hid the entire package of cocaine outside my apartment in the bushes and called a well-known junkie to pick it up. How stupid could I have been to call a junkie to pick up my stash.

Carlos

There was another drug dealer named Carlos, who worked on the Florida State campus. He had been trying to get me to his house for months. Carlos was known for getting women high and then taking advantage of them. Carlos had added my roommate to his list, and she hung out there often.

My roommate, Debra, was a very sharp young lady, but she was streetwise on another level. Her game was to seduce men for money and drugs. If you had nothing to offer Debra, she did not have time for you. She was a bottom-line person and was more hardhearted than I was. Carlos begged her to get me to his house.

It was a period of time when Danny seemed to be trying to get things together with the girl he was living with, so I started to see other guys. They bored me, because all the while I kept seeing Danny's face. When Debra called me to come to Carlos' house and smoke cocaine, I had a young man at my apartment. This young man was a pharmacist and drove an awesome Porsche.

Although at first I wasn't interested in Debra's offer to join her in smoking cocaine, I eventually gave in to her peer pressure. The guy with me begged me not to go, insisting that I did not realize what I was about to get into. Despite his plea, I made him drop me off at Carlos' house.

Once we entered the driveway, the pharmacist shocked me by begging me to take him in. It turned out that he himself was an undercover junkie. Undercover junkies are the worst kind. They hide behind their profession, under the disguise of being doctors, lawyers, pharmacists and even preachers. No different from the street junkies, they are just "rock stars" with an occupation.

Many people testify that they've been delivered from drugs, when actually they haven't been. I've watched preachers start churches, prosper and then backslide to the crack houses after 10 years. Why? Because the strongman or the root of addiction had not been dealt with. The strongman is good at lying dormant until the precise moment when he can snatch you back again. The worst thing you ever want to see is a "formerly delivered" junkie. Once returning to the pigpen of drug addiction, the seven-more spoken of in Matthew 12:45 is something difficult to reckon with.

I walked into Carlos' house and found my roommate with no panties on and a white girl with no bra. The entire environment seemed strange to me, and I asked Debra why she was naked. They just put a pipe to my mouth and asked me whether I felt anything. I did not feel a thing and was getting quite uncomfortable about the entire ordeal.

I called Danny to come over, and he and Carlos hit it off fine, because they were in the same game. They had a lot in common, even in their desire for me. I never felt what everybody else felt when smoking cocaine; it did not turn me on. Carlos and I quickly became friends and business partners in the drug game, but the devil would not let him rest about having control over me. He often told me he wanted to "really" get me high. I told him I wanted to, but it did not work like that for me.

Overdose

One day I was washing my clothes at Carlos' house, and he asked me if I was ready to "really" get high. I said yes, so he took the mirror of the dresser and taught me how to make crack from raw cocaine powder. We cooked at least a half ounce of cocaine, and he took me into the bathroom to hit it. We did not smoke from cans or hitters like they have today. We had cases of manufactured glass pipes that we had gotten through the black market. He instructed me to draw from the pipe as hard as I could, as he had packed its head with raw crack.

If you have ever been delivered from cocaine and are reading this now, you need to bind the spirit of *pharmakeia* now, because a taste may try to come into your mouth and the devil may try to make you remember how good cocaine made you feel. The devil is a liar. He never reminds you of the bad, only the good. People are not losing jobs, houses and families over a bad feeling. Cocaine makes your flesh feel good. The feeling is short and quick and does not last for more than a moment. The aftereffects when you run out are incredibly tormenting.

I know that no agony can compare to hell, because God made it for torment. But the next thing to hell, as far as I am concerned, is to be a junkie without a fix. The pleasurable part of smoking cocaine is so minute in comparison to the long-lasting torment. Cocaine is a god to its prisoners, and it lords over everything in your life because it demands to be served.

When Carlos put that pipe to my mouth, all I remember is that I could not talk. Everything around me seemed to be moving, as if a movie camera was spinning around on its tripod. When I finally spoke, my words were slurred and did not make sense. My body responded as if I were having a stroke. My first "real" hit of crack and I had overdosed.

I passed out and Carlos laid me in his bed. He was stretching over me to finally have his way sexually, when to his surprise, I woke up and looked up at him. With a frightened expression, I asked him, "Who are you?" He tried to tell me he was Carlos, but my mind was gone. I did not recognize him, and I screamed RAPE at the top of my voice.

I wrestled with Carlos from the back of his house to the front door. He was paranoid about the police, so he had several locks, chains and bolts on the door. I was as strong as an ox and literally out of my mind. I got to the last lock on the door, and was about to run outside like a wild woman. Suddenly my mind partially came back, which must have been the hand of the Lord upon me. Relieved that I was returning to my right mind, Carlos dropped to his knees and said, "Thank you, Jesus," not even knowing the One he so adamantly gave thanks to.

If the police had stumbled upon us that night, we would have been put away for a long time. Up until then, the closest I came to getting arrested was when I took a small package of cocaine to Henry to snort while he was in jail. I drove to the police station outside Gainesville, Florida, and my trunk was filled with ounces of dope and cases of drug paraphernalia. When I pulled my identification out, marijuana paper fell on the floor. That was probable cause to search me, and all they needed was a dog to sniff for the dope in my panties.

There was no explanation for how I avoided going to jail for that incident, except that God spared me. Amazingly, I've never been arrested a day in my life. I give this testimony to the glory of God, because if anybody deserved to do jail time, I did. I believe there are two reasons God did not give me a "prison ministry" on the other side: homosexuality and suicide.

I never was tempted to participate in homosexuality, and I did not understand the spirit behind the act. I avoided it because it was not my cup of tea. Having been an athlete, a drug addict, and a member of the military would ordinarily entail some kind of homosexual exposure. My testimony, however, is that I was never exposed to this demon. Yet I am on assignment from the Lord to cast it out of the church.

I also always said that if I ever went to jail, I would kill myself. My mind was made up. Fortunately, God will not allow you to go through more than you can handle.

Down to a Whole New Level

I wish I could report that I learned my lesson from my crack overdose with Carlos and my narrow escape from being raped. Instead, I went to another level in abusing drugs. The demon that I had entertained and controlled now had control of me. Despite the awful experience when I overdosed, I would have given my life to feel it all again.

On the streets they would have said I had a "wall-banger." This means to reach the ultimate high. You only get one wall-banger in an addiction, and then you spend the rest of your time trying to obtain a feeling you will never feel again. Nothing ever again is like that first "real" hit, because it is the bait to snare you. Once you're caught in the web of addiction, the devil does not owe you anything. You're not a challenge to him anymore.

I realize now that I was trying to prove something to myself and others, but all the while I was playing the devil's game. Satan likes challenges! The more you confess being sold out to Jesus, the better a catch you are to him. That is why the Bible says a double-minded person cannot have anything from God (Jam. 1:6-8). Our attitude must be "for God I live, and for God I die."

Double-mindedness gives room to the enemy. It opens doors that will be difficult to close. Steadfastness and stability are crucial elements in deliverance, keeping the devil from moving us out of place and stringing us along toward ever-increasing bondage.

Chapter 10
BACK WITH DANNY

The young lady Danny was living with threatened to leave and take the baby if he did not change his lifestyle. Threatening to take his child was her main tactic to control him, for she knew that the baby was the only thing holding their relationship together. Her mother had often worked witchcraft on men to get them to fall in love with her, and the same technique had been used to lure Danny.

Danny was dating many women, as he always had. One of the young ladies he was dating was a fashion model and had strange, green eyes. She won a beauty contest at one of the nation's most popular black colleges. She was very conceited, but she loved the ground Danny walked on.

Danny's relationship with me was quite different from the other ladies he dated. I knew all his girlfriends, and Danny and I often talked about them. By the time the other ladies found out about me, Danny and I were living together.

A few weeks before we moved in together, the model with the green eyes came to town looking for Danny. Somehow I talked him into letting me pick her up to talk with her. As I drove her to meet Danny, she cursed me out and called me all kinds of names. All I could hear in my ear was my grandmother saying, "Strike first and ask questions later!"

Instead of taking her to Danny, as I promised, I detoured and drove her to my apartment. She was a big woman and I had not fought in a while, but I was happy to use the occasion to brush up on my skills. As I approached the outside of the door, I yelled to my roommate to move the coffee table. As the beauty queen entered the house, I struck her like a mad woman. We fought until she cried uncle, and I went into the bathroom to get alcohol for her wounds. We could talk now! Although I clearly got the best of her, she almost bit off the side of my left breast. I was sore and did not want to fight anymore, and she definitely didn't want to pick any more fights with me.

Danny and I laughed about the incident, and the bathing beauty went back to Miami where she belonged. Danny and I moved into a beautiful wooden house with a screened-in front porch. Though he was a drug dealer, he was a country boy at heart. He was my best friend and I was his. People would always ask him why he lived with "that wild little girl," and he would answer, "That's my partner!"

Danny and I were both addicted to cocaine by now, and the more money we made, the more cocaine we smoked. There are no real friends in a crack house, but Danny and I loved each other so much that we would have given each other our last hit. This may sound silly, but it has got to be a miracle for a junkie to be willing to give anybody his last hit.

Life in a Crack House

Our resources soon reached zero. When you are in a business and you consume more than you profit, you will eventually end up with a negative financial situation. One Christmas season it was so cold in Tallahassee that the pipes broke. We had no heat or food. We did not even have a Christmas tree. I was walking past a church the week before Christmas and a fully decorated tree was lying on the trash pile. Why would a tree be thrown away one week before Christmas? I pulled it home and loved on it.

Danny managed to come up with something to eat—string beans, which I never liked. But under the circumstances those were the best stringed beans I'd ever had. I usually was happy even in the worst conditions, but in my heart something said, "Danny will soon leave." Every time he walked out the door, I was gripped by the fear that he would never return. His best friend lived with us in our wooden house, but Danny and I eventually moved into our own apartment and I felt closer to him than ever before.

Times were hard financially in the wooden house, but when we moved to the apartment on Pensacola Street, the spiritual opposition was unbelievable. Sometimes I felt like I was losing my mind when Danny left me alone. I loved him intensely, and despite our lifestyle was hoping to soon be able to have my son live with us.

For the first time, we allowed our apartment to become a crack house. It was full of Jamaicans, Haitians, Cubans or whoever came through the city with the goods. One night there were dope dealers of every kind in the house, comparing their products. They had manufactured pipes, scales, test tubes and bottles of grain alcohol.

At such times, I couldn't shake the premonition of the vice squad kicking our door in. If that happened, I knew I couldn't flush all those tools down the toilet. Every time I got high, I saw a newspaper headline that said, **"Track Star Busted for Cocaine."** This was my unshakable fear. If the vice squad would have ever kicked the door in, I knew I would have had a heart attack right there.

I had met my match. That white horse, that girl, that fire, whatever they called it…cocaine is a god and it must be served. Who serves cocaine? Whoever is foolish enough to let it in the house and dare think it will serve them. To sell drugs on the streets is even called "serving." Cocaine serves no one! There are two kinds of people who deal with it, pushers and junkies. Both are servants to this master called cocaine.

A life in the cocaine game can only end up three ways: prison, insanity or death. It is a one-way road that leads inevitably to a dead end. Jesus is the only exit on this hell highway. Cocaine has broken the best. Many have tried to make the cocaine game a lifestyle for eternity. They like being self-employed and not having to answer to anyone. There may not be a physical person for you to answer to, but you will answer to Baalzebub, the lord of the flies.

Cocaine will make you do to your family and loved ones what only a maggot would do. Your immediate overseer is mammon, because fast riches are a part of the game. Ten years in the life of a cocaine dealer is like 70 years on a regular job. If you beat the legal system, AIDS will run you down, and if you escape AIDS, addiction will destroy you. Sleep doesn't come easily, and peace is hard to find. If that weren't enough, there are thieves and robbers waiting for your vulnerable moment so they can take your stuff—and they will kill you to get it. No one breaks the mold of cocaine: either you fit in or you pay the incredible price of getting out.

As I watched the dealers compare their dope, I began to hear the vice squad outside the door. They were cocking their weapons and giving each other signals. I knew I had to get out of that house, even if I had to leave Danny to do it. Fear gripped me to the point that I could hardly breathe. Frantically, I begged Danny to get me out of the house.

As we drove down the street, police cars were surrounding us. I was so scared. I had the love of my life, Danny, drop me off to the house of a guy who we knew liked me. When I came down off my trip and realized that the whole episode was only a nightmarish mirage, I started crying for the guy to take me back to Danny.

I was losing my mind. There was no vice squad, no voices, no police cars, but it seemed so real. The demons were playing a game, and I was the joystick. I could tell by the way Danny was looking at me that he was ready to do something new, but I would not say it from my lips.

When you run out of crack, a common reaction is to think you see it on the carpet. I used to crawl on my knees for hours, collecting cotton in hopes that a rock had fallen from the pipe. Another reaction is to look out the window in a paranoid manner. Although Danny usually acted pretty cool when he got high, I noticed that he was now on the floor and at the window, just like me. Who was going to look out for us now? Cocaine had its hook in both of us. One night Danny got so high that he tried to hide from the police in the apartment pool, holding onto the sides with the water up to his neck.

Heartbreak

My hardest times were when Danny went to visit his son. I did not know much about praying, but every time he drove away I hoped he would come back. Other than Danny, I had literally cut myself off from everything and everybody. My goal in life was to get at least a quarter of an ounce to smoke a day. I could no longer get high off of what I started out with.

We started hanging out with a pro basketball player who would come by to get me high when Danny was out of town. He just needed a place to hide out. The last time he left, he told me I was too bad off and needed to slow down. No one wanted to get high with me anymore, because they said I would "blow their high." Everyone enjoyed smoking cocaine, but I took one hit and started hearing voices and even grabbing other people's cocaine and flushing it down the toilet. I was really "out there" and had no idea how to come back in.

One summer night, the voice I always heard got so loud that I put my back against the front door and began to scream for my imaginary police to come and get me. Tenants were sleeping outside by the pool with sheets over them to ward off the bugs. Finally, I ran to the pool area and snatched a sheet off of a tenant and yelled, "I knew you were out here!" Embarrassed and frightened, I ran back to my spot on the window, holding my hands over my ears to stop the police from calling me out of the house. If I ever needed to be committed somewhere, it was not a joke this time.

Danny and I used to look at MTV all day long, and we hooked the television to the stereo for better sound. Rock music did something to us. We would jump around the house like fools, but only rock and roll gave us this effect. Why was this? Most of my life I didn't even like Rock and Roll. I was not in Oregon anymore, and now had a choice of stations.

Rock music and drugs walk hand and hand. We could not stand any noise while we were smoking cocaine, but if we listened to rock music, it gave us an extra incentive to get some dope. I will never forget a song called "Free Base." Those were the only words, over and over again. When I listened to that song, I had to have some cocaine. Free base is nothing but crack cocaine, but there is nothing free about it.

Danny and I sat down to have a serious talk one day. We concluded that we could not keep living the same way as we had been. The police were hot on our trail. Another close accomplice had been busted on the city bus. Danny said we had to run, and I was willing to run anywhere with him. If the police would have ever busted us, I don't think I could have turned state's evidence against him. He and Mike-Mike were all I had.

Danny broke the situation down and explained that we had to go in separate directions. When he announced that he was leaving the next day, my breath left my body. I called my Aunt Lillie Mae and begged her to tell him not to leave me. I told her how I was on drugs and could not make it without him. I never cried so hard in my life.

Nothing I said was able to change Danny's course. He dropped me off to the same guy's house where I went the night I was paranoid. Danny drove off in a Chevrolet truck packed with his belongings, but I only took a bag of clothes. He left me on a Wednesday, and by Friday I was so sick I had to see a doctor. The doctor told me I was pregnant. This was a little comfort, because I felt like it might make a difference.

The next day I called Danny's grandfather, and his exact words were, "He went to the wedding." It took me a while to catch on, and I had to ask him whose wedding it was. When he told me it was Danny's wedding, I did not need to commit suicide, because I felt as if I died at that moment. For days I sat gazing at nothing, taking breaks only to cry. The only way I made it through the first week was by realizing it was best for him because, after all, I was "just a rock star."

The guy I was living with said he had always loved me. He was a clean-cut guy with his own construction business. I knew that he would take good care of me, but I did not want to be taken care of—I just wanted to die. I could only stay with this young man temporarily, because the bitterness in me affected anyone I was around. He was too nice and did not deserve it.

Back to French Town

I moved around the corner from the French Town, where I could easily walk to get a fix. At first I felt like I had nothing to lose. A big-time drug dealer named Frank was always after me, and he took me under his wing. He kept me high, put me in fancy hotels, bought me things, and promised to help me with Danny's baby. Since I had no concept of true royalty, all this made me feel like a queen.

I was concerned about smoking cocaine while I was pregnant, but I knew another rock star who had smoked dope nine months and her baby was very healthy. Every time I considered trying to quit during my pregnancy, the devil showed me how well her baby had turned out.

Frank got me an apartment, and I lived like a vampire—up mostly during the night. If someone knocked on my door before noon, I thought they were crazy. My normal time for getting up was 3 p.m. I would eat a small meal at this time, and then hit the streets to set up something for the midnight hour. I used to call midnight the witching hour. Everybody wanted to be settled into whatever dirt they were getting into by midnight.

After giving my heart to Jesus, I realized that from midnight to daybreak is a very important time to get on the wall of intercession. This is when many dope addicts are calling on God. They may not know Jesus yet, but there are lots of prayers such as, "God, please let me come down this time, and I will never do it again." Every rock star prays this prayer.

My appearance started to decline. I was not gaining weight. I started dressing without care for how I looked. Colors did not matter. Bathing was not a priority. I began to take on the physical appearance of what I really was: a rock star.

Men would walk up to me and tell me how I used to look good. They would go on to tell me how bad I looked now. When I ran to the mirror, the devil told me they were lying and that I still looked good. I found myself with men I could never have imagined being with. I eventually stopped crying over Danny, but my heart became calloused and hard. I had no friends. I had seen supposed friends walk out on me, and I began to put my trust in no one.

Rock Bottom

The demonic attacks while I was high got worse. I did not have one associate, male or female. I only dealt with people for the purpose of getting a fix. One morning before daybreak, I ran upstairs to my neighbor's place to tell him someone was in my apartment. He looked at me as if he did not believe me. He would not let me in, nor would he come down to help me.

I went back to my apartment wondering why my neighbor treated me that way. The devil reminded me, "Nobody trusts a rock star. Everybody knows you are a junkie, and they won't believe a word you say. Besides, nobody is in the house anyway but you and me."

I knew I had hit rock bottom, and it was time to go back to Jacksonville. No one knew what I was going through. I called one of my saved friends and was crying as I told her about Danny leaving me, marrying someone else, and leaving me pregnant. To my shock, she and her sister burst out laughing at me. Though they did not actually say it, I could hear them thinking, *Not you, the track star, homecoming queen and president of the Student Council…How did you wind up here, going from "track star" to "crack star"?* I was not even embarrassed, because the hurt went beyond shame. Another girlfriend and one of my old coaches picked up whatever was left of me and got me out of Tallahassee.

When I returned home, I moved in with my father's first wife. I always kept in contact with her, and she told me I reminded her of my youngest brother. He was killed uptown while snorting cocaine and prostituting women. He was my favorite brother, and it was hard to believe he was gone.

My brother had been a fighter like no one I had ever seen. Once when a drunk old man called me a name, my brother savagely attacked and beat him until he was bloody. I begged him to stop and had to pull him off the old man, who had put up no resistance at all. My brother kicked the old man one last time, and cursing he said, "This old man lives by the laws of the streets. He didn't have to be here, but as long as he's here, he has to suffer the consequences!" A few years later, my brother was gunned down with six bullets, two blocks away from where he beat the old man. When you live by the laws of the streets, you will surely die by them one day.

New Scenery, Same Script

I went from the streets of Tallahassee to the streets of Jacksonville. The only difference in my circumstances was that I visited with my son periodically and had responsibilities at my stepmother's house. We had one big cleanup day, and the rest of the week we did brief cleaning. She never charged me a dime for living with her.

The places you hang out will determine the kinds of people you meet. I loved to hang out at my father's club, where the sissies performed every Wednesday night. One day I met a guy there named "Scorpion." He was the biggest con man uptown, and was commonly known as the "Jack Man." He would rob his momma to get a hit. He was a cocaine addict, but he also got a thrill in masterminding robberies, burglaries and even murders. When he walked into a room, his fierce mentality to care about no one brought fear to many. People did not want to be bothered with him, because his presence always meant trouble.

I have a brother who was my father's oldest child from another woman. He lived with cross-dressing homosexual men and at other times slept in abandoned buildings. To my knowledge, he still maintains this lifestyle. Even when I had a warm bed to go home to, I would periodically spend the night in abandoned buildings with Scorpion and my brother.

For the first time in my life, my father rebuked me. He said if I was hanging around Scorpion, he knew I was on skid row. Scorpion was ugly, dirty and treated me badly, but something drew me to him anyway. I moved in with his father and he used me to get dope. Sometimes the devil would get in him and tell me, "Look at you…You ain't nothin' but a junky…just another rock star!"

Six months had elapsed since Danny left, and I never thought about him. One day, he called my stepmother's house, but I could not even work up the nerve to ask him why he left. Nor did I discuss my baby or his marriage. Later I found out that he would not have believed me about the baby anyway. People had told him lies, claiming that I was only pretending to be pregnant.

Instead of talking with Danny, I hung up the phone like it was a wrong number, and then hit the streets. I suppressed the love I had for him and chose not to meditate on the memories of our happy times together. I had to move on with my life. I had no desire to see Danny and convinced myself that I had no interest in even knowing what he was doing.

What's That Smell?

Days later, my room began to have an awful smell. I was looking for a dead rat, but couldn't find it. I fell asleep and was awakened by the sweat of a high fever. I went to the emergency room six-months pregnant, and found out that the baby had died at two months. I was so busy trying to get a hit; I did not realize that my baby was dead and rotting inside me. That's what was smelling. I cried for a while and was on the streets the next day.

I went to work as a gymnastics trainer for a Russian family. Even though they didn't know me, they gave me money for a 1979 Chrysler LeBaron. No one had ever given me anything but cocaine. I did gymnastics in the daytime and hung out with Scorpion at night. When I got my first check, Scorpion snatched the money from my hands and told me he was going to flip it to make drug transactions.

A murderous spirit came on me at that point. I borrowed a pistol and went back on the street, threatening to kill Scorpion. The look in my eyes let him know that I meant business. I embarrassed the jack man in front of all his friends, and I knew I had to make a move.

I ran to the Army recruiting office and told them I needed the first assignment they had. Within a few days, I was at the reception station on orders to South Carolina for basic training. Grace had run out for me to live on the streets.

Chapter 11
IN THE ARMY NOW

Basic training changed my life. I did eight weeks at Fort Jackson in South Carolina. The number eight is often seen in the Bible as the number for new beginnings. Truly I was at a point where I needed to try something new.

When I stepped off the cattle truck, which transported us like animals to our destination, I could not even spell the word "discipline." It is amazing how God will use natural tools to make a spiritual difference in our lives. I could not relate to the things of the Spirit, so God used the military to put me on the right track.

The drill sergeants scared the life out of most of the women in my group. To me they looked like what I called a bunch of L-7's (when you put it together you came up with a square). I had no respect for their authority, and they knew it. The first day, the head drill sergeant walked up to me and said, "Private, you think you're bad, but I'm gonna break you!" All I could think was that if what I already been through had not broken me, he wouldn't be able to either.

I had a bad reputation in the platoon. I got in trouble every other day for fighting someone in the bathroom. I could not stand a snitch, and when I caught one of them in the bathroom I would slap them around. Yet no matter how much I threatened people, they still told on me.

Boot camp became so monotonous: "Private Parrish, drop! Get up! Get down!" They could not break me with physical punishment, because I was physically fit. When I could not do any more pushups, I simply stopped. Most of the young ladies did not have the revelation that you can only do so many pushups, and when you run out of gas, pull over and rest.

Bowed by Unbroken

Drill sergeants are trained to mess with your mind, but I had just come out of the devil's basic training, so to me this was a breeze. If Scorpion, Killer and Razor did not break me on the streets, a drill sergeant did not have a chance. My immediate drill sergeant hated my guts. This was not just a part of the game played with every recruit—he really had a problem with me. He called me nappy head, told me my breath stunk, and cursed me like a sailor. One day I rolled my eyes at him, and he and I got chest-to-chest cursing each other out. I waited for him to hit me and he waited for me to hit him.

Halfway thru training, I got tendonitis in my left ankle and they put a cast on my leg up to my knee. I never ran for physical training during my entire eight weeks, so I stayed in the barracks and slept. This was unheard of. None of the women asked me to clean any of the common areas, because my grandmother's belligerent nature would rise up in me and I would want to curse and fight. They just left me alone rather than to deal with the verbal abuse.

Throughout the battalion I got a reputation as a soldier who would not break. So wherever I went, the drill sergeants tried to gang up on me. They would put me on the wall and search me like the police. When I got the cast on my leg, they could not make me do pushups, so they made me stand on one leg with both arms holding my M-16 in the air. That meant lifting my heavy casted leg.

KP (Kitchen Police) was a place for people who got in trouble, but I felt like a part of the permanent staff. A group of them would see me in the distance and yell, "Halt, get up against the wall!" Just about every day, they threatened to send me to jail, but somehow it never happened.

Two weeks before graduation, my favorite drill sergeant sarcastically reminded me that because of my limitations with my cast, I would never be able to pass the physical required to get out of basic training. I would have to be "recycled." All this time, I thought I would soon be out of basic training, but now it looked like I would be his pawn for eight more weeks.

However, another nice drill sergeant caught me sleeping on guard duty, and he gave me a helpful suggestion as he walked me around to check all the bunks. He told me that if my cast slipped off while I was taking a shower, I could try to pass my physical fitness test. At first I could not understand what he was recommending, for I couldn't figure out how that long cast would slip off my leg in the shower. Seeing that I still was missing the point, he finally said, "Cut the cast off and take your physical fitness test."

I followed his instructions. I scored 100 out of a possible 100 points on my test. After that, I started treating people better and even helped my bunkmates with chores. Something was happening to me, and I found myself wanting to be a part of what was going on. The drill sergeant called me into his office and told me I had been a sharp soldier for the past two weeks. He even apologized to me, saying he should have made me squad or platoon leader. His theory was that I then would have been more open to his training, and the women under me would have been well-supervised.

I went to advanced training with a new attitude. I still had a lot to learn about following orders, but the key was "I was willing." The principles in the Bible are true whether we know them or not, and God was teaching me an important truth: *"If you are willing and obedient, you shall eat of the good of the land"* (Is. 1:19).

Back on the Track

My first duty station was in Germany. I learned as much as I could about the military, but after hours I hung out in the party scene. When I met with the company commander for my first interview, he asked me what my goals were while being overseas. Before I could even think about it, I blurted out, "Sir, I'm gonna be the fastest female military sprinter in Europe!"

Within a year I was not only the fastest female in Europe, I was the fastest in the entire military. My All-Army track status followed me everywhere I went. I always got easy duty assignments that would allow me time to train. I got to know the Department of the Army Athletic Staff, and they kept close watch on my off-season activities. I took pride in being a sharp soldier, and made sure I met the requirements for a promotion.

In four years I became a Staff Sergeant (E-6) in the United States Army. The average time that it takes to make this rank is ten years, and God blessed me to reach this status in less than half the time. I did not even know the Lord, but He knew me before I was formed in my mother's womb. He knew me in the crack house and He knew me on the winner's podium. I'm glad that when I did not even take time to tell Him thank you for waking me up in the morning, He looked past my faults and saw my needs.

Mike-Mike finally moved back with me. I was financially stable enough to provide for him like I never imagined. I purchased my first home, paid off my first car, and kept money in the bank and in my pocket. By the fifth of each month, every bill was paid. Mike-Mike lived like children I had only seen on television.

The club scene got old, and I had so many boyfriends for the first five years of the military that I could not even count them. I did not have a lot of boyfriends at any one time, for the turn-over rate was high. After my relationship ended with Danny, my favorite slogan was "I don't love hard anymore." If a guy rubbed me wrong in any way, I simply went on to the next phase.

One guy took me to Denmark to marry him. He was an All-American basketball player and was several years younger than I was. He was handsome, had a promising future, and loved me. The day before the wedding, I gave him the engagement ring back and apologized. We returned to Germany where a big reception had been planned, only to cancel the party. People were upset with me, but I knew my heart was not fully in it.

Married!

I moved back to the states, where I was stationed in Georgia. Danny visited me there. He seemed to be successful in life, and I was happy for him. I spent a day with him and showed him around the army installation. If I still loved him, I could not tell it. All I could think was that he belonged to somebody else and I hoped he would be happy. My emotions were unmoved, but I still knew he was my best friend.

I met a young man who I took an interest in, and we got married. We seemed very close, and he was good for Mike. The day I got married I almost missed the ceremony. I was standing in the grocery store line at 5:15 p.m., when Mike-Mike reminded me I was getting married at 5:30. My husband-to-be was dressed in a nice outfit, but I wore a pair of old jeans because I did not have time to change.

As we approached the judge, I reminded him that I did believe in divorce if it did not work out. In my mind the ceremony was a "swearing in." What a vow! Circumstances had rushed our decision to get married. We were living together, and I received orders to go back to Germany. We had to make a quick decision to separate or to get married. The reason the divorce rate is so high in the military is because the financial system is designed to benefit married couples. Instead of holy matrimony, couples often have an arrangement based mostly on financial considerations. I was faced with an either/or situation, and I took the easiest way out…I thought.

Six months before I flew to Germany, the Lord started to get my attention. My neighbor was a saved lady, but she never had food to feed her children. She would come over and say, "Well, I guess I'll put my children to bed without dinner." I did not know anything about being saved, but I figured if being saved meant I had to starve, I did not want it. I would pack bags of groceries and feed her and her children. I did not try to figure it out.

I was having bad dreams all the time, particularly whenever Mike-Mike and I were home alone. I would see little imps pulling him out of my bed, and when I got up to check on him, he would be sleepwalking. These recurring dreams were so real that I would often make him sleep with me so I could put one arm around him and hold him in the bed. One night as I was walking from my room to his, I saw hundreds of the little imps having sexual orgies on my floor. I had to step over them to get to Mike's room. I never told anyone, because I already had a record at the crazy house and did not want to add to it.

'For Sale'—and Redeemed

On a beautiful spring day, an old man came to my house because of the "For Sale" sign I had put in the yard. He told me he was interested in buying my house, and then said as he walked through the inside that God was telling him, "This is the house!"

I was following the man with my legal papers so we could talk business, but he just walking and praying.

Finally he said, "God wants to use your house to shelter and feed the homeless."

I thought, *God can use it for whatever He wants to use it for, as long as He can pay it off!* Although the man kept saying, "This is the house!," he afterwards rode his old bike down the road, never to be seen again. It really did not make sense to use my house as a shelter for the homeless anyway, for it was in the middle of a residential neighborhood.

I never thought twice about this strange visitation, but six months later my entire household was saved. It was not until years later that I realized it was not a physical house that God wanted, but He wanted to live on the inside of *me.*

My conversion was initiated by watching a movie called "A Thief in the Night." This movie rocked my world, and I wasn't good for anything but Jesus. I found out that I was on my way to hell and urgently needed to change course. The first thing I thought about was my friend who laughed at me when I told her Danny left me. She did lead me in the sinner's prayer at that time, and I had forgotten all about it. I am so glad Jesus did not forget.

I went to Germany a new creature in Christ Jesus, but was in need of much deliverance. When I arrived at my duty station, Allah, Jehovah and the Mormons were all waiting on me.

Chapter 12
A BABE IN CHRIST

I did not understand a lot about the Christian life, but I knew that Jesus was the only one who gave me peace. For the first time, I did not have to depend on my skills and abilities. I had found someone who loved me unconditionally, just as I was.

Becoming a part of a church was a different matter, though. I tried attending a holiness church, but because of how I looked, they politely asked me to leave. God delivered me of drugs, cursing, fighting and many other things like a bolt of lightning. But some things, like the way I dressed or my worldly manner-isms, came off in layers. Although I was saved, I still had a strong, worldly flavor in my life, especially in how I dressed.

I have never been one to give up, so I tried another church under the same denomination. I was so glad to be saved, and I wanted the world to know that Jesus was lord of my life. The church service went well, and some of the sisters invited me over for dinner. However, they told me to bring a change of clothes.

'Looking Saved'

I decided that I wanted to look *really* saved when I had dinner with the sisters, so I wore a pair of lo-o-o-ong shorts. The shorts were to my knees, but were still very tight. Hey, this was a leaps-and-bounds improvement for me. My usual summer attire would have given them a heart attack. I was trying so hard to fit in, and based on where I had come from, I was doing fine.

We have to be very careful not to judge people for where they are in God. We have no idea what the Lord has delivered them from. Our hangups and idiosyncrasies can tear down the work God has begun in them.

My hair was cut in a punk-rock style with a variety of different colors, but I felt like I could deal with that in time. Apparently the sisters did not agree. Whenever I sat down next to one of them, they immediately moved. They treated me so badly that I began to smell under my arms to see if I stunk. Though they looked so holy, I could see straight through them.

I went to the sister who invited me to church and asked her if I should leave. With sorrow in her eyes, she said it might be best for me to go. After she quickly walked away and left me standing alone, I got my things and escorted myself to the door. Not only did they neglect to feed me, but no one even showed me how to get home. I was in a small town in a foreign country and was not familiar with the area.

I cried all the way home, praying that God would lead me home safely. Hungry and lost in a foreign country, I felt like a foreigner in the body of Christ. I had never been a church-goer before, so there was much I did not know. I had to depend on God for everything. Nothing I knew from my previous life applied to the spiritual realm, because my life had been based on worldly and fleshly things. I had to start like a little baby and learn everything all over again.

'Turned on' to Jesus

The simplest things in God were so important to me. I had something inside me that every born-again believer should have: a desire to know the whole truth. In the world I used to like my cocaine raw. Cocaine used to be "my thang," and it turned me on. Now Jesus is "my thang," because He turns me on. I do not want another spirit, something that would adulterate or water down the truth. I like my God "raw," and I refuse to settle for anything less.

This is important, because only the truth will make us free. As the end-time remnant of God, we don't have time for frivolous distractions and hindrances. The ultimate purpose of adulteration of the truth is to mix it with leaven. A little leaven will leaven the whole truth! (See 1 Cor. 5:6.)

Truth is preached every day, but many are still in bondage and cannot receive it. Yet the Bible says that whenever light comes in, darkness has to flee, because light devastates darkness. To devastate means to completely destroy. If the Son has truly made you free, you will be free indeed, because the enemies of your soul will be devastated! (Jn. 3:36)

I was living for Jesus the best I knew how. I received orders to return to Presidio, California, to train for track season. A special bonus was that I had been chosen to be the sprint coach. In years past, I was the fastest woman in all four armed forces, but my contentious attitude had gained me a reputation. A season did not go by without me cursing someone out. One year I picked up a pair of starting blocks and started swinging them at a 220-pound male athlete.

The major who was in charge of overseeing the team had overlooked these incidents and restricted me to my room. I was only allowed to leave for track practice. There were times when my teammates had to bring my meals to my room. This behavior had gone on for years. They put up with my fits because I could win the gold.

A New Woman

In 1988 I stepped on the plane to training camp for the first time with Jesus leading the way. The first team meeting was very dramatic for me. For years I had lived like a heathen, and now I had to tell all the athletes that I was saved. We usually picked on all the so-called "saved" athletes. How would the team accept me?

I stood up to announce that the Air Force had recruited a group of college athletes. I explained to them that we had a great challenge for the upcoming season. I closed out my speech by saying, "through Christ Jesus, we can do all things!" The bus was silent. Many looked around to make sure that what they heard was right. Many shook their heads and said they would believe it when they saw it in my life. They were not willing to receive my word alone that I was saved—I had to show them something!

After a few weeks, everybody knew my conversion was legitimate. They watched me like a hawk. They listened for the foul language to start running from my mouth. People even tried to pick arguments with me to instigate a fight. In no time, 50% of the team was saved. We met to pray at 7 p.m. every night in the basement. We knew nothing about the Bible, so everyone took turns reading a verse and then we prayed prayers that I know touched the heart of God.

We spent several weeks looking for a church, but from what we could tell, Jesus was not in any of the churches we visited. We went to several denominations "looking for Jesus," but it seemed that we were "looking for love (and Jesus) in all the wrong places." Even when we went to the big cathedrals, we could not find Him there.

The last girl to get saved was a javelin thrower, and she told us she had found a church that Jesus was in. It was a small church that had a seating capacity of no more than 75-80 people. The pastor was in his mid-twenties, but he had a female evangelist speaking. She prophesied that there were three young women in the congregation who God was calling to the fivefold ministry. Nothing in me said that I was one of them, so I looked around to see who it could be. My natural mind could not fathom God using a person like me.

Shadowed by the Devil

The closer I got to God, the more opposition I felt. I could not put my finger on it, but I felt like somebody was following me around. One day instead of leading my team to church, I let them go alone. I went to the club, played bingo, drank alcohol and smoked a cigarette. What was happening to me? I was out of control of my decision-making process. Even the unsaved Kim would not have gone to the club a few days before the big meet.

It was as though some force was leading my steps, and before long the devil personally introduced himself to me. I had promised the javelin thrower that I would buy her a dress for church when she got saved. But to my surprise, when my pay stub came it said, "No pay due."

How was I going to live? My son was in Germany living with a family while I trained. I began to feel heavy about the situation, and I fell asleep hopeless. Yet as I slept, Jesus hovered above me. He talked to me and told me He loved me and would take care of me. He wrapped me in His arms and told me that everything would be all right.

The Lord talked with me much of the night, and then I had a dream. I saw a woman with a big check standing in the financial aid office. The check was huge and it had my name written on it in bold print. As I got up from the dream, I was late for the finance appointment I had scheduled. The financial aid office was in the building next to my barracks, and as I ran into the office door I was shocked to see the same woman who was in the dream.

When I told the woman my name, she said she had a check for me. As I walked out of the door with the check in my hand, I realized that it was not even payday. The military sometimes would issue pay statements before the money was actually distributed. The devil was telling me I would not get paid, but God had paid me early.

Lessons in Faith

For the first six months of being saved and paying my tithes, I had to fight for my paycheck every month. It is quite ironic for a military person to have to worry about a check. The military has a ruler spirit presiding over it, whereby it tries to present itself as your provider. It assures you of what we called "three hots and a cot." This meant three meals and a place to lay your head at night.

In my case, though, my check was being garnished for a debt I incurred before yoking up with Uncle Sam. As I traveled around the world in the military, every payday told the same story: "No Pay Due." Those in the finance office would tell me there was nothing they could do for me, and would ask me to leave. Nevertheless, I sat quietly in my chair, reading Kenneth Hagin books on faith and praying in tongues under my breath. For six months, despite how crazy people thought I was, I never argued and I never left without full pay.

I will never forget the day God delivered me from this situation. I walked into the finance office in Fort Stewart, Georgia. The officer recognized me and said, "You can flip on your head today, but you have no check due and you will not get one." I sat down and began to read my books and pray as usual. One of my friends came in and tried to convince me that I was making a fool out of myself. She encouraged me to get a loan from the Army Emergency Relief. I told her that as a tither and a child of the King, I would accept nothing less than what God said I could have.

The Lord had instructed me how to walk through this dry season, but every devil in hell was on the scene to ensure that I would not pass the test. Five minutes before the office closed for the day, the phone rang and a lady on the other end said she was calling in reference to Kimberly Parrish's case. I heard the finance officer say in amazement, "She is in our office now!" The lady asked to speak to me.

When I put my ear to the phone, she said words that shook my very soul: "JESUS IS LORD!" She was calling from the Department of the Army Finance Office in Virginia. She said the Lord had been dealing with her concerning my situation. She explained that the debt had been forgiven and I would not have to deal with the situation anymore. Hallelujah...I passed the test!

If we pass the tests we go through in life, it will be just as God told Israel: The enemies we see today we shall see no more (Ex. 14:13). When I received my L.E.S. (Leave and Earnings Statement), my heart rejoiced as I saw typed on a Department of the Army Form "Debt Forgiven...Jesus Is Lord!" I still have that paper today. Every now and then I look at it to remind me of my tailor-made miracle from God. What God has for me...IT IS FOR ME! The devil is not the only one who has people strategically positioned in high places. To God be the glory!

Chapter 13
TESTED AGAIN

The Bible says that the enemy comes immediately to steal the word that has been sown on our hearts. The devil clearly did not like my new faith and endurance in God. He could not make me bow with a natural challenge such as financial distress, so he came at me with a spirit of witchcraft.

One of the other coaches hated me and wanted nothing to do with God. When I lived for the devil, he practically kissed the ground I walked on. But when I sold out to Jesus, he despised my very presence. As I would lead athletes to the Lord and pray for them, like a wolf he tried to devour the fruit at its inception.

He had never been a good athlete. When I was a recruit on the track team, he would always get cut from the team and sent back to his unit. He definitely wasn't a good coach either, but somehow he convinced the Department of the Army to give him a break. He was a "yes sir" boy, and seemed to just be filling a slot so someone else could run the team through him.

You have to be watchful of people who want what you have. This man was ruled by a spirit of failure and was jealous of my leadership ability and gift of being a champion. The spirit of failure worked with rejection and insecurity to lead him head-first into rebellion. Spirits of jealousy and coveting are obsessive spirits and will make people cross lines spiritually.

This is the kind of mind-set that motivates mass murderers and serial killers. Their obsession starts with thoughts like, "Since no one is paying any attention to me, I will kill as many people as I can. *Then* they will pay attention to me!" A person with this type of personality can entertain demons for selfish motives and be quickly escorted into the realm of the demonic.

Witchcraft is amazingly subtle in its inception. It is deceptive in nature and operates best behind closed doors. The biggest closed door of witchcraft is ignorance. The word ignorance simply means a lack of knowledge. God says in His Word that a lack of knowledge is what kills His people (Hos. 4:6). To perish means to be wiped out or destroyed. We have many casualties in the body of Christ because of ignorance.

Proverbs 1:29 describes people who hate knowledge and do not choose the fear of the Lord. Psalms 25:14 says the secret of the Lord is with those who fear Him. Those who fear God know that witchcraft is God's enemy. Satan is the god of this world, and to be a friend of the world is to be a friend of the devil, because he is the god of witchcraft.

Attacked at Night

I went to bed early one night and was awakened at 3 a.m. by a sharp pain in my side. Because of the intensity of my workouts, I rarely got up before 5:30 a.m.. I went to the bathroom, but as I walked the pain got more intense.

Although I did not understand anything concerning witchcraft at that time in my Christian life, I knew something was wrong with me, and I knew it was not natural. Something supernatural was going on, but at first I had no idea what it was.

Still bent over in pain, I happened to pass by the door of the young man who hated me. With a smirk on his face, he stood at the door and looked at me, never even asking what was wrong. By this time I was yelling at the top of my voice for someone to get me to the hospital. I felt like I was in labor, but the pain was even more severe than I could remember labor having been.

At the emergency room I screamed for about an hour, begging my roommate to do something to help me. I could see her compassion, but she felt helpless to ease my suffering. My roommate, Porsche, was the only young lady who had not given her life to Jesus, but her mother was a praying woman. Porsche gently put her hand on my head and simply said, "In the name of Jesus."

The doctor had taken tests, and he called me to his office to give me an evil report of my condition. Before the doctor dropped the bomb on me, he wanted to run more tests. Praise God, the next round of tests came out negative. The doctor would not tell me his first finding, because his only explanation was that somehow the x-ray wasn't mine!

There was no way that two x-rays could look so different. One x-ray was cursed and the other was blessed. I quickly learned that satan could not curse whom God had blessed. This drew much attention, but the medical staff cited human error rather than giving God the glory for another miracle.

I asked my roommate why she laid hands on me, and she did not even understand why she had done it. I learned that God will take the foolish to confound the wise, and there is a way that seems right to a man but the end of it is death. At the time I happened to be in San Francisco, one of the satanic capitals of the world. San Francisco was the home of the main church of satan in the United States at that time.

In addition to being attacked by witchcraft, I also had opened doors to demonic influences because I was not totally delivered. I was taking anabolic steroids for the first time. I was strong as an ox, but some injuries kept me from ever using that strength in competition. Another female athlete who was a world-class competitor took me to what was called a "head shop." Now I know it to be a store to buy artifacts for witchcraft. I walked in for a minute, but I could not stay inside. This store sold satanic bibles and all kinds of other creepy items. At the time I never wondered why she would go into a place like that. Later God revealed to me that she was not only on anabolic steroids like I was, but she was praying to satan to give her supernatural athletic ability.

I definitely had no interest in serving the devil, but I was very ignorant about the many ways he can get a foothold. I took frequent trips to the Chinese shops for acupuncture. Even the wildest athletes knew something was wrong with acupuncture. I just wanted healthy legs and I would have done anything short of serving the devil to get them. What I did not have a revelation of was that by such activities I was serving satan, whether I realized it or not.

Preparing for Combat

My experience with the attack from witchcraft showed me that I needed to be better prepared for satan's onslaughts. Some great lessons in "combat readiness" were learned from my training in the military.

Formations in the Army were at 6 a.m., even for those on the track team. Every good soldier had to learn to rise early. There is a worldly cliché that "The early bird gets the worm." To me that "worm" represents God's provision and whatever is needed to make it through the day. When David was in the wilderness of Judah, he told God, *"Early will I seek thee."* Isaiah said his soul desired God in the night, but the spirit within sought God *early* (Is. 26:9).

The word "early" means "initially, at the beginning, or in advance." In other words, we have to be ahead of the devil. It is not necessary that God will wake you up at 5 a.m. every morning—the key word is discipline. Every disciple of Jesus must have discipline. Disciple means follower and discipline means to be trained to the point where self-control develops and you will accomplish the mission at any cost.

In the military, the key word for every disciplined soldier is "combat ready." This means to maintain a high level of effectiveness. This effectiveness is only achieved when we understand and walk in the calling we have been given. This is why the Navy Seals or the Green Berets are so respected. They specialize in particular types of warfare.

This is also the power of the strongman. He is a specialist in whatever field he is called to. Demons are highly disciplined, and they do not cross lines. They are called to garrison or guard the captive so he or she may not be released from the stronghold. For example, a spirit of lust will not cross the lines of a spirit of error. Each strongman is focused on being an expert in his area of operation. If the fivefold ministry gifts and all the individual soldiers in the body of Christ would be focused on their individual missions, the phrase "fitly joined together" would become a reality.

Taming the tongue is another key to combat readiness. Psalms 34:11-14 reads:

> *Come, ye children, hearken unto me. I teach you the fear of the Lord.*
> *What man is he that desireth life, and loveth many days, that he may see good?*
> *Keep thy tongue from the evil, and thy lips from speaking guile.*
> *Depart from evil, and do good, seek peace, and pursue it.*

David wrote this psalm when he was fleeing from his rebellious son, Absalom. He started the psalm by saying he would bless the Lord at all times and that God's praises would continually be in his mouth. The psalm states that the fear of the Lord is separating ourselves from evil. The initial step in separating from evil is to guard our tongue. There is life and death in the power of the tongue, and out of it we can either bless or curse.

The devil shoots his main blows against the mind of the born-again believer. He understands that if our mind ever gets renewed, he does not have a chance. Isaiah 26:3 says God will keep us in perfect peace if our mind is stayed on Him. Peace means to have an undisturbed state of mind or to be free from conflict. When our mind is renewed, it will no longer be the devil's playground. We will be able to cast our cares on the Lord and recognize that the battle is His.

Walking Away

After the attack on my body, I was healed and ready to run. The Air Force, Marines and Navy came to Presidio that year to compete. The night before the meet, God strongly told me to leave San Francisco. I could hear Him very clearly bidding me to leave. In the natural it sounded crazy, but somehow I felt that I was not dealing with a natural situation.

I got my roommate up and explained to her that I had to leave. She thought I was crazy. It was so difficult walking away from track and field at the peak of my career. In New Mexico in 1988 I had already qualified for the Olympic Trials. I was winning the final race of the 100m and pulled a muscle 10 yards before the finish line.

That scene used to play over and over in my head. The young lady who passed me won the race and broke the record. What a blow! What would my time have been? The enemy often haunted me with "what if's."

It is a terrible thing to know you had the potential but were never able to bring it to pass. Because of the bondages in my life, I never ran to my full potential. I was always hindered and distracted from being the best I could be.

Even as I was walking away from track, I did not question God. No matter how much it hurt, I realized He knew what was best for me. The devil told me that I could stay with it and "run for Jesus." People always asked why I couldn't continue. I understand now that it was because track was my god. It was similar to why Danny had to leave me: He was my god.

The Bible says you cannot serve two gods (see Matt. 6:24, Ex. 20:3). If you try clinging to two gods, it says you will end up hating one and loving the other. My discipline as an athlete and discipline to God would have warred against each other. It would have been a "good thing" to do but not a "God thing." Only what you truly do for God will last. God removed all the other "gods" from my life so He could be Lord.

The Bible says that Hagar despised Sarah after Isaac was born. If you do anything out of the will of God, it will oppose or despise the promise of God for your life. I had to learn to wait on God's "Isaac," because the promise is in him only. Those who wait on the Lord will not be put to shame (see Rom. 10:11)

Dealing with the Devil

I went home on leave for a few days and spent time at my father's house. My stepmother had been saved and filled with the Holy Ghost. In the past she and I used to smoke dope together and hang out at the sissy show. Seeing the change in her lifestyle had really had an effect on me. She may not have led me in the sinner's prayer, but I am grateful that she planted a seed.

My stepmother casually mentioned that they had cast demons out of a woman at her church. After hearing that, I followed her around all day, begging her to tell me demons weren't real. If demons were real, then all the dreams of the demons and Mike-Mike were not dreams after all.

Despite my efforts to dissuade her, my stepmother wouldn't back down from her belief in the reality of demons. It all came together now: the attack on my body, the voices in the crack house, and the little imps that pulled Mike-Mike from the bed were all demons. I made up my mind at that point that the devil would not torment me anymore. I decided to retaliate.

When I flew back to my duty station, the devil was waiting on me at the airport. It seemed as if a dark cloud was following me around. I could literally sense an evil presence. When I got back to the military installation, I tried to hang out with the "saved" girls, but it did not work. There was something about them that kept me from getting close to them.

I was still smoking, and a curse word would slip out every now and then. I asked them what was different about them and me. They replied, "We have the Holy Ghost." I asked them how they knew they were filled with the Holy Ghost. Their response was so shallow that I knew they were only mimicking what they had heard or read somewhere. I needed the whole truth on the matter, and they did not seem to have it. I confronted them on how they could have something real, if they could not explain it to me.

I had only been back on normal duty for two weeks, when my stepmother called and said she was going to "Daddy Hagin's

Camp Meeting" in a few days. At the time, I carried a case of Kenneth Hagin books with me everywhere I went. Every spare moment, I was studying his Bible teachings. It took a lot of self-control not to read at the red lights while I was driving. I knew I wanted whatever this Hagin guy had.

I told my stepmother I would see her at Hagin's meetings, and she said I was crazy. Most people had planned all year for this trip, and she did not think I could jump on the boat at the last minute. What she did not understand was that I *had* to get there. All of my natural circumstances said "no," but something inside me insisted "yes."

I had a negative 21 days of leave, meaning that I owed the army 21 days. Yet my first sergeant approved me for an additional 20 days of leave. I had been back in the country just three days from 90 days of training and leave. It would have taken 1½ years for me to accrue this time again. The army paid for my ticket, which was to be deducted from my next paycheck. God is so good that the 20-day leave never showed up on my pay stubs, nor was the cost of the plane ticket deducted.

However, even as God blessed, the demonic opposition got stronger. When I was sleeping in my bed a few days before leaving for the camp meeting, long, wiry monkey arms started coming from under all four sides of the bed. These arms began strapping me down to the bed. As I called on Jesus, I heard a voice yell, "Shut up," as one of the arms covered my mouth.

Even though my flesh was still pinned to the bed, my spirit man took over and continued calling on Jesus. While this battle was raging, the lights in my house were clicking off and on. Although the devil did not bother me so much when I first got saved, he was now showing his face in an all-out attack when I pursued deliverance and the filling of the Holy Spirit.

After this experience, a spirit of fear came upon me, and I was afraid to stay at home alone. I started sleeping on the floor of my soldiers' barracks. But I proclaimed to the Christian girls I had met on post that when I returned from the United States this time, I would be speaking in tongues and sleeping in my own bed.

However, it was a battle all the way. The BMW I was driving to the airport in Germany broke down. Running out of time to catch my plane, I had to hitchhike to the airport. When I sent someone to pick up the BMW along the road and tow it for service, it worked fine for them. Upon arriving in the states, I had a Mercedes to ride in—but it broke down too! Clearly the Lord was planning something special for me at the camp meeting, and the devil was doing everything he could to prevent it from happening.

Chapter 14
FREE INDEED

The camp meeting was awesome. I had never seen anything like it. After the first night I was tired from jet lag and attempted to go to bed. My roommate told me they were having prayer on the eighth floor. Even as I put on my pajamas, I heard a voice say, "Go." I went in with a young lady from Jacksonville who I had met on the trip. Something in me was afraid to go in that room, but I felt safe with this new friend. This young lady was Pastor Sirretta Williams, who is now a pastor at my church.

When I walked into the room, I felt God's presence like never before. What was this language they prayed in? They would even sing in this language, and as everybody sang, it sounded like one voice. I had to have it.

These people were Baptists, and even new believers know that Baptists don't pray in tongues. Yet God said that in the last days He would pour out His Spirit on all flesh. That included the Baptists, and even me. A young man gave a tongue and inter-pretation, saying "an unclean spirit is among us." As hard as it was to accept, I knew he referring to me. I was the one with a demon.

Some people try to play the dumb role and pretend they do not need deliverance. Although you may not be able to put your finger on it, when you are in bondage you know something is wrong. I knew I was the one with the unclean spirit, and the man told me to step in the middle of where everyone was standing. Stepping forth was an acknowledgment that I had a problem.

Like I always say, "If you have a devil problem, you need a Jesus answer." That night I was delivered from demons and filled with Holy Ghost with the evidence of speaking in other tongues. I have been reproducing others like me ever since.

On Fire

When I returned to Germany I was lit up like a firecracker. Everything in my life did a turn around, but more important than anything, I refused to allow the devil to torment me again. I had a revelation of who satan was and that I had power over him.

God began to use me. I founded a prison ministry and barracks ministry in Germany, and many souls were saved. However, I was not received well by the local churches. The things I walked in seemed foreign to them, and my presence seemed to intimidate them. I did not know any better. I just believed and practiced what the Bible said.

After being physically put out of two churches, God gave me a church home. It was the largest charismatic church in Frankfurt. The pastor supported me in every way. I met many Christian friends and we were like family. After six months, I was put in charge of the teenagers and was allowed to preach to them every Sunday. I had the liberty to cast out devils and get the teens filled with the Spirit as God led.

I then received military orders that sent me to a German community an hour away, and I started attending the full gospel service at the military installation. The chaplain was a black, female major, and she walked in the power of the Holy Ghost. Again I was put over the teen ministry and children's church. I was even made the supervisor of three volunteers.

The chaplain encouraged my zeal in God, and she was an example in my life of walking in spiritual authority. One Christmas, she flew my mentor, Pastor Bea, to Germany to do a revival on post. Pastor Bea came to Germany with Sirretta and we terrorized satan for two weeks. The hordes of hell didn't stand a chance.

We loved God, knew our authority in the Holy Ghost, and cast out devils! People began to call us demon busters. I remember times when Bea and Sirretta would be at the beauty parlor with plastic bags over their heads, and when they heard of someone needing demons cast out they would immediately leave the parlor and go to minister with the bags still on their heads. Pastor Bea taught us everything she knew. We went to prisons, crack houses and many hardcore areas where most church members would not go.

Pastor Bea had a flavor in the spirit that I have never seen in another person. When she spoke, demons would shake in their boots. Sirretta and I loved Pastor Bea so much. People talked about us because of the way we served her and sacrificed for her. We were her armorbearers in every sense of the word. When I was with her, my mind never wandered on "my ministry." There was an intense desire in me to make sure that *her* ministry went forth.

Demon Busters on the Loose

Although I was about to achieve a E-7 rank in only eight years, God prompted me to leave the military on an early discharge. Everyone thought I was crazy for walking out on such a promising military career, but I knew that God had something better.

The Demon Busters came into agreement to start a nonprofit organization to feed the homeless in Jacksonville. Pastor Bea had already been feeding the homeless in the park on Saturdays for years. The name of the new ministry was "Feed My Sheep."

I will never forget how Pastor Bea, Sirretta and myself became true friends. When we came together for prayer and ministry, we walked in a threefold cord that prompted the supernatural. Once we went to one of the most dangerous housing projects in Jacksonville. We always joked about how the freaks came out at night, so we would often start our outreaches after 11 p.m. This night we started about midnight.

Business was booming for satan that night, but God moved mightily to set people free. We led people to Jesus, cast out devils, and even prayed for people to be filled with the Holy Ghost. The corner that we were standing on was on the path to the dope man's house. People on their way to get cocaine and marijuana were going back home with their money in their pockets, speaking in tongues.

We rejoiced in the great victory over darkness that we witnessed. The only problem was that the dope man did not rejoice. He sent two thugs to shut us down, and they were not planing to do it politely. We could hear them saying, "Get those b——'s as they came near us. We began to pray in tongues, and the guys seemed to run into an invisible wall. As I think back, it looked like a Roadrunner cartoon. We could not see anyone in the natural, but something was throwing these guys around like pancakes. They ran away from us in terror, holding their hands over their ears.

I can remember thinking, "This is better than the sissy show!" I knew that the greater one was on the inside of me, but it was also a comfort to see the outward manifestation of God's supernatural protection. As time went by, I became more sold out to God. The more I experienced his miracles, the more I had to have all of Him.

A Surprising Call from God

One day Pastor Bea invited me to give my testimony at a women's meeting in one of the local churches. Pastor Bea led the praise and worship, and was over the women's ministry. I enjoyed attending the services at this ministry when I was in the states.

The pastor was a young man who played football for the Denver Broncos. I could really relate to him, and I considered him my home pastor. Pastor Don always made himself available, and he often gave testimony in the pulpit of what God had done in my life. My conversion was so drastic that it appeared as if I changed from Mr. Hyde to Dr. Jekyll. Everyone wanted to hear my testimony. Maybe this led Pastor Bea to put me on the women's program that Saturday, but the Holy Spirit had another plan.

I arrived a little early to pray with the intercessors, and Pastor Bea walked up to me looking as beautiful and elegant as she always had. But the words she spoke put me in temporary shock. She told me that the speaker had not shown up. I told her I was happy to pray concerning the situation, but I still did not catch on to what she was saying. What did the speaker not showing up have to do with me?

The room was filled with women expecting to hear a word from the Lord, and I asked Pastor Bea what they were going to do. She looked at me and said, "You're it!" I could not believe what I was hearing. Fear gripped my soul. I was not a preacher and could hardly find the books of the Bible. And I had less than 15 minutes to prepare!

Despite all the objections I felt in my heart, my lips would not come together to form the word "no." I had to do it, but I needed help. I looked around the room and saw the gentle face of the same lady who went in the room with me to get delivered at the camp meeting: Sirretta.

I asked Sirretta to go outside with me, not daring to speak until we were in a place where no one else could hear our conversation. I walked her down the stairs, outside the building, and to the back of the parking lot. I looked her straight in the eyes and said, "They want me to be the speaker!" She looked at me with almost no emotion and responded, "Baby, everything's gonna be all right. Let's pray." We prayed and I trusted her faith, because God had just blown my mind.

When they introduced me, I stood at the podium, read a scripture, and opened my mouth to address the women. As I started to speak, the people could not stop laughing. It was going great! This was easier than I thought, and I was enjoying myself until the Holy Spirit told me to lay hands on the people.

If I were sitting in the congregation that day I do not believe I would have answered my own altar call. I told the people that God wanted me to lay hands on them and that I had never done it before. I also told them they did not have to come if they didn't want to. I was hoping no one would respond, so it would all be over.

One lady walked up. She was Sirretta's mother. I laid my hands on her and she fell to the floor. I stopped and looked at my hand. I could not believe what had happened. I had seen this type of manifestation of the Spirit before, but now I knew it was real. The power of God had moved through me.

A shocking thing happened next. Pastor Bea came up and stood in front of me for prayer. What is wrong with this picture? This was one of the most powerful evangelists in the city, and she wanted me to pray for her. When my hand made a connection with her head, she fell under God's power also. That day I ministered to approximately 150 women. Demons manifested, people were filled with the Spirit, and most of all, God was getting the glory. Truly, no one could take the credit for what happened with those women.

A Whole New Season

The most important thing about this experience was that it convinced me I had a call of God on my life—a call that was requiring me to go to another level. I now understood with certainty that God could use anybody He wanted to use. Like never before, I saw the truth of Luke 19:40 in action: *"And He answered and said unto them, I tell you that, if these should hold their peace, the stones would immediately cry out."* Though I was the least qualified to preach that day, when the others didn't make themselves available, God used a stone.

Many believers have become too comfortable on their pews. There are prostitutes or drug dealers who may one day knock them off of their seats in order to get close to God. Those saved from life on the streets are hungry for more of God. People want Jesus. If the evangelists will not win souls, the prostitutes will. When pastors get weary in well doing, the drug dealers will feed God's sheep. The rocks will cry out!

This word for "stone" or "rock" in the Greek is *lithos,* and it means "a stumbling stone, obstacle or impediment." Someone with a speech impediment does not have clear articulation. They do not have the natural power to speak properly. A rock also represents a lifeless, empty vessel. To sum it up, God is looking for those who do not have it all together, so He can use them for His glory With all the military training, education and natural abilities that God had blessed me with, there was nothing that could have prepared me to speak that day. I had to totally depend on Him and recognize that it is the anointing that destroys the yokes that have held people in bondage.

When I arrived back in Frankfurt, I had gone to a new phase in my life. I had to get to know God and this power that was now flowing through me. I spent long hours with God for the next couple of years. He was consistently speaking to me as if I were talking to my neighbor. I talked to Him early in the morning, during my lunch breaks, and late at night. I could not get enough of His presence.

God had blessed me with a Bible study in the barracks, which we called the Upper Room. I never intended to preach at the meetings, but would recruit other preachers to hold the services. I saw my role as gathering the crowd, which I was clearly gifted to do. Yet many times when I scheduled preachers to speak, they would call me the night before and say that the Lord had told them *I* was supposed to be the one speaking.

The Lord had anointed me in such a way that people starting to say I was a witch. This rumor did not come through the heathen but through Christians. At this time, 95% of the people I ministered to had never known Christ. In contrast, those in the religious community "knew too much" to let a person like me pray for them. God spoke to me and said He was shutting down the Bible study in the barracks. I really struggled with giving it up, but I knew it was His ministry, not mine. Many other adventures in faith were still ahead.

Chapter 15
DESERT STORM

War was declared in the Persian Gulf, and Operation Desert Storm changed all of our lives. Fortunately, the Lord moved me to a new duty position as the supply sergeant for the 10th Armored Division Band. Two weeks after the move, my old company was given orders to depart for Saudi Arabia. Being spared duty in Desert Storm was a blessing in more ways than one.

For years I had been in custody battles over my son. Mike-Mike's father claimed that my military career would not allow me to provide an adequate lifestyle. After I finally won the custody battle, I was about to be deployed to the battlefield in Saudi Arabia and was required by law to sign my child over to the nearest relative. Things looked very promising for Michael's father, but God had promised me that I would be able to raise my child in the way he should go.

Once the soldiers knew they were being deployed to war, Resa and I were the only ones who continued to come to the Bible studies. Even though God had told me He was closing down the studies, I wanted to continue them until everyone left for the war. By this time most people were trying to spend time with their families or just party and drink their fears away. They became subject to whatever the enemy could conjure up to keep them from worshiping God. But Resa and I were faithful every Wednesday night. I would preach to her, and she would preach to me.

The Spirit of God had captured my life in such a way that even war could not take away my joy. The Lord had made promises to me before I found out that my company was about to deploy. These promises did not line up with going to Saudi Arabia and signing my son over to his father. As I walked across the parking lot for my interview to be transferred to the 10th Armor Division Band, the Spirit of God spoke, "Go with this new position! Your present company is going somewhere and you are not to go with them!"

That was it! I had my answer. God did not want me to deploy. His peace surrounded my mind and I knew I was in His perfect will. No devil, war or rank could override God's promise to me. After I transferred to the new division, it received deployment orders too. Even so, I was convinced the Lord had promised to keep me from being sent to war.

I shared what God had promised me with a few of my military friends, and word quickly spread around the post that I said my God would not let me go to war. I was the laughingstock of the compound. People I did not even know began to crack jokes about "my God" keeping me from going to war.

The Favor of the Lord

God gave me favor during pre-deployment, and I was in charge of thousands of dollars of materials needed to equip the soldiers for battle. I was the supply sergeant, and it was my job to provide supplies, all the way from snacks to mosquito nets. During that time the Holy Spirit would give me revelations about procedures to help my commander prepare for wartime.

One day I passed by a soldier named Corporal Day, who was standing in the lobby crying. When I approached him, he explained that his wife had left him and wanted a divorce. I began to laugh, and told him his problem wasn't big at all. I explained to him that his situation was small in God's eyes and that God could easily deal with his wife's heart. He accepted

Jesus Christ as His Lord and Savior, and was filled with the Holy Spirit with the evidence of speaking in other tongues. That night his wife returned home and met with the corporal and me to pray. The corporal was knocked off his feet by the power of God.

Soon after Corporal Day's conversion, the commander made him my driver. This enabled us to spend many hours together praying in tongues. One day as the corporal and I were driving to a small town in Germany to pick up supplies, he confronted me about something that was bothering him: Why was everyone saying I thought my God would keep me from going to war? I smiled at the corporal and explained that the rumor was true: God did tell me I was not going to war.

Corporal Day then asked if I could pray that God would keep him from going to war also. For some unexplained reason, I said yes. I explained to the corporal that God honors childlike faith and that if we agreed together with the right motives, He would answer our prayer.

One week later, a letter was published throughout the company that listed the personnel who would not deploy. Included on that list were my name, the corporal's and an administrative clerk. Out of 10,000 soldiers, we were the only ones on the list who were not exempted because of being pregnant or disabled. God had shown Himself mighty on our behalf.

Resa's Miracle

Resa called me one night with excitement in her voice. She explained that God had spoken to her that she was not to deploy to Saudi Arabia. Before the war was declared, she had orders to West Point Academy and she felt as though the enemy was trying to rob her. It was snowing that night, and I asked her to bring certain documents to my home so I could prepare an appeal of her deployment. I had never done this type of document before, but I knew I could do it if it was God's will for her to go to West Point.

On the way to my house, Resa got in a car accident and called me from the emergency room. The Holy Spirit quickened my spirit and I knew the devil was trying to block God's plan. When the devil lifts his head, he often ends up confirming God's will. Now I knew I was on the right track, and I pursued the completion of the documents with fervency. However, when we submitted the documents, they were immediately rejected. Not only did the Army reject our request, but it also recommended that Resa be released from the military early. I knew that this was a form of retaliation, but my faith went to another level because I did not forget the will of God in this situation. The case was not closed, as I was soon to discover.

Despite many trials, my time overseas was the most awesome time in God I have ever experienced. I spent hours upon hours communing with the Lord, going to realms in God where few others dared go. My lunch breaks where spent evangelizing soldiers. I would pray about which table to sit at and claim the soul of the person sitting with me. I would often take soldiers to my room in the barracks, where I would cast devils out and pray for them to be filled with the Holy Spirit.

One day I was not paying attention to where I would sit for lunch. I plopped down at a table and looked up to see a colonel sitting across from me. I was immediately frustrated, because I felt like he was not ready to be witnessed to. I did not want to offend him by moving, so I sat there to complete my lunch. I had been leading at least three to four people to the Lord daily, and was irritated that my time was being wasted in sitting with someone who had no interest in the gospel.

Little did I know that God had another plan. The Word of the Lord says our ways are not His ways and our thoughts are not His thoughts (Is. 55:9). I introduced myself to the colonel and remained cordial. As I was speaking to him, his brass rank pin seemed to shine like gold. I noticed the name on his name tag, and it seemed oddly familiar.

Then I remembered who he was. My heart started racing. This could not be him. I was sitting at the table with the commanding officer who rejected Resa's appeal! I was lit up with the anointing and could sense the favor of God on me. After I explained Resa's entire situation, the colonel reviewed her papers again and sent them back to her approved. What an awesome God we serve! To my knowledge, Resa was the only one who changed duty stations during deployment to war. It was absolutely unheard of. But all things are possible through Christ Jesus.

Change of Plans?

By the time the troops were loading equipment for deployment, Corporal Day was declining in his spiritual discipline. It seemed that once he had gotten what he wanted from God, he was content to lie back in apathy. I warned him that he had to continue to pray in the Spirit and give God the glory in his life. He just indifferently nodded his head and carried on with his complacent attitude.

Two weeks before deployment, I was ordered to appear before the company commander. He was a Mormon and knew I was radically sold out to Jesus. Yet God would use him to provide all I needed to minister to the soldiers. We had an auditorium in our company that seated 500 people. He would allow me to use the auditorium to have Christian conferences, without ever complaining that I was using the government's facility for religious purposes.

As I approached the commander's office, Corporal Day was passing by, cursing God. He looked me in the face and said he knew the Christian life was all a lie. He had orders to Saudi Arabia. He yelled that my orders were next to his—he would see me in Saudi. I stood before the commander, not knowing what to say or do. He briefed me that I had orders to Saudi and needed to sign the papers to send my son back to the U.S.

As I reached for the pen, the Holy Spirit said loudly, "Do not sign those papers!" But what did God expect me to do? Did I have to go to jail for disobeying a lawful order? I did the only thing I knew to do at the time: I asked the commander if I could be excused to go to the bathroom. On they way to the bathroom the voice of God told me to bind the devil. Satan and I met face-to-face at the latrine that day. I prayed with such fervency that I took a physical stance as though I was in starting blocks in a race.

I did not know how to bind demonic ranks, so my exact prayer was this, "Devil I bind you, your mama, your daddy and your entire generation. Loose me in Jesus name!" This prayer may not make sense theologically, but I did not need anything to make sense. I needed a miracle! God says He will take the foolish things to confound the wise.

The hordes of hell were coming up against my promise. Satan was using high-level rank in the natural, coupled with demonic infiltration, to take me out of God's perfect will. I did not know much about spiritual warfare then; I just knew God. Today, I recognize this attacking spirit as the spirit of *Haman*. This spirit operates through high-ranking positions in the natural. Though the influence people see is one of a natural source, behind the scenes *Jezebel*, *Python* and *Kronos* (father time/death spirit) operate as a threefold cord against God's people and His will for their lives. *Jezebel* controls the will, *Python* confines the movement, and *Kronos* conforms God's people to the ways of the world.

The only way to deal with the spirit of Haman is by doing spiritual warfare. This type of warfare takes dedication to the purpose of God and a high level of spiritual disciple. With these two key factors effectively working, the gallows that Haman builds for God's people will ultimately cause his own demise.

I left my prayer closet in that latrine with another level of peace. Nothing else mattered, because I had done my part. I felt like Esther: "If I die, I die!" When I stood before the commander's desk the second time, he leaned over and whispered, "Don't tell anybody, but you are not going." Those words sounded like music to my ears. It was not so much that I didn't want to be deployed; my praise report was that HE FULFILLED HIS PROMISE!

As the other soldiers deployed, I was given a new job. I had the honor of escorting V.I.P.'s to the air base to wave goodbye to troops as their planes departed. All my peers who made jokes about "my God" watched from the plane as I waved them off with a Holy Ghost smile. I did not rub it in with my peers, but I made sure that the devils never forgot the victory I had won over them.

I know that many soldiers sincerely prayed to be spared from the deployment, and I asked God why He chose to keep me and Resa back and not the others. The Lord reminded me of the times we went to the Bible study alone, despite the circumstances. The Holy Spirit also spoke to my heart with a soft, gentle voice and said, "You were the only ones who would believe that I would do it."

Chapter 16
HAND-TO-HAND COMBAT

All of the companies came together to form a rear detachment, and I was one the highest-ranking females left. Resa had one rank above mine, but she deployed to New York. The rear detachment was mostly filled with pregnant or injured soldiers. A spirit of death swept through the barracks, and a couple of babies died of crib death.

God united me with a soldier named Private Lucy James. Private James had an introverted personality and was not a very attractive young lady. I witnessed to her and prayed for her to be filled with the Holy Spirit. God enabled her to open up to me, and we became very close. Private James had a unique ability to see into the spiritual realm. She saw demons and angels, and had dreams and open visions.

One day I received an emergency call to go to the military hospital. Sergeant Wynn, a female staff sergeant, requested that I come and pray for her baby. I was very surprised, because this female sergeant had often criticized me and called me a religious fanatic. When I entered the hospital room, the first sergeant of my company and several soldiers were present. The first sergeant was an ordained deacon in one of the churches that had asked me to leave.

As Private James and I entered, a silence filled the room. Sergeant Wynn looked pale, and she was leaning over a very sick baby with tubes in its head. She had not eaten for three days, because she feared her baby was next to die. She stood up and repented for all she had said about me. She said she did not understand a lot about spiritual things, but she knew that God answered my prayers. She wanted me to pray for her baby, and she personally wanted whatever I had in the Lord.

The other soldiers in the room did not think too well of her words, but I began to give God the glory. I took authority in that room and boldly suggested that we joined hands in prayer. Hesitantly, the first sergeant and soldiers joined us in prayer. As I began to pray in the Spirit, Sergeant Wynn fell to the floor. I thought she had fallen under the power of God, but that was not the case. When I reached down to pray for her, she looked up at me with her face cracked and her eyes rolling back into her head. A ruff man's voice came out of her, shouting mockingly, "Hallelujah! Thank you, Jesus!"

This scene was so frightening that the first sergeant and soldiers ran out the door. A couple of them could not get out fast enough, so they stood trembling, with their backs against the wall. Every one of them professed to be a Christian. For some reason I was not afraid. Although I have always been afraid of scary movies, the state of this woman did not move me to fear.

As I looked down at Sergeant Wynn's demon-possessed expressions, I heard the voice of God proclaim, "In my name they shall cast out devils!" Pastor Bea and I had never dealt with anything like this. We just commanded the devil to leave by faith. I did not realize he could take over a person in such a way. As I commanded the demons to loose this woman, her body began to respond. By this time, the nurses' station was alerted that a problem was occurring in the room. The focus was no longer on the baby; now the mom was in trouble.

The Holy Spirit quickened my spirit that the hospital staff would admit Sergeant Wynn to the psychiatric ward for a nervous breakdown. God commanded, "Do not let them!" I realized that the woman was unconscious and that devils were using her body. I walked her down several floors and out to the parking lot. As I walked her toward my car, her head was rolling around on her body like a paraplegic. She was growling and incoherent.

I had never seen a demonic manifestation like this before. I wanted to take her home and practice casting out this kind of devil. As I took her to my car, I would periodically whisper in her ear, "Wait until I get you to my house." I was naive as to what I was dealing with, and didn't stop to consider that the devils heard me.

After I managed to get Sergeant Wynn to my car, I was startled a loud voice that said, "Halt!" Two male soldiers who were much bigger than me and who had much more rank took her from my car and back into the emergency room. Under the circumstances, I felt like my mission was over, but Private James had a vision from God. She said God had told her we were not yet finished ministering to Sergeant Wynn, and that we could not leave the hospital.

I believed that Private James had heard from God, but my rank was on the line and I needed another witness. Before I could get this thought out of my mind, a nurse came out of the room Sergeant Wynn was in and asked us to guard her. We were dressed in duty uniform and it was the ideal situation.

Private James and I laughed out loud, for we knew the devil had been defeated again. I walked in the room and jokingly said, "We're back!" The demons began to cry out. Sergeant Wynn's legs began to bicycle as if she was running. She sat up like a stiff board and became silent. As I looked into her eyes, a horrible voice slowly released the words, "I know you!" I looked at Private James and exclaimed, "Isn't that a scripture from the Bible?" I still considered myself a spiritual novice, yet the demons recognized who I was in Christ.

As I think back on this incident, I know the gates of hell shook that day. God initiated me as an official demon buster. The breakthrough came when I had a vision of placing my hand on Sergeant Wynn's back. As I obeyed the vision, the demons screamed that it was getting hot inside her body. They cried out that they were burning and left her body as I commanded them in Jesus' name. Sergeant Wynn returned to normal and never remembered anything that had happened. She was never admitted to the psychiatric ward.

Backlash

This incident took place on Friday, and on Monday morning I was summoned to the rear detachment first sergeant's office. He was one of the people who ran out of the room when the demon manifested in Sergeant Wynn. He was my immediate supervisor and had been my number one critic on post. He was a deacon at the church that I know now had all the manifestations of a religious demon. This church was a part of a very popular denomination, which I will not mention at this time.

This first sergeant commanded me to get at attention and began to read me my rights for a court-martial procedure. I was put on barracks arrest and told to stand by as I was being considered for an Article XV charge. This meant that I faced reduction in rank, a dishonorable discharge, or even military prison. I did not know what I had done. I was told not to pray in tongues, not to touch and agree with anyone in prayer, and not to lay hands on anyone.

The spirits of *Hymenaeus* and *Leviathan* were so thick in his neck that a spirit of stupor had come upon him. The first sergeant was trying to charge me with fault for Sergeant Wynn's incident. He literally called me a witch and told me to stand by for further counsel. The enemy was setting up this soldier to lose natural and spiritual rank. As I sat outside his door, he called clerk after clerk with manual after manual to find an official charge. I prayed fervent prayers, loosing confusion to the enemy's camp. I did not understand all the details of military law, but I could not see what I had done illegally.

When I finally stood before the first sergeant for him to read my charges, he stated that I was being charged with the following:

1. The anointing of oil
2. The laying on of hands
3. Praying in tongues.

As I heard the charges, a big smile broke out on my face as I almost burst out into laughter. God had loosed confusion. I do not think the first sergeant realized how silly his charges sounded. I informed him that he was coming up against my religious rights, and if he could not come up with better charges than that, I would counteract with a complaint for harassment. Despite this, the charges went through the legal channels, only to be thrown out in the end.

To Saudi After All

The Persian Gulf War was getting serious. We were on curfew and Mike had to stay with one of our church members. One week before the fighting started, God spoke to my heart to go to Saudi Arabia. Isn't that just like God, to cancel my orders and then ask me to go with no orders? I had to obey God at any cost, but how do you deploy to the battlefront with no orders? There were several reasons God wanted me to go to Saudi Arabia, but it was mainly to take biblical materials.

Smuggling Bible materials into a Muslim country is not a very safe thing to do, but I had a vision from God. If God could give me orders to go, He would keep me safe as I took the materials. I decided to share my vision with Kenneth Hagin Ministries. Dr. Hagin had never heard of me, but I told him that God had led me to contact him. He sent several thousand tracts and Bible study materials. Through Kenneth Hagin Ministries and the Army chaplain department, I was equipped to evangelize, but I still needed orders to the Middle East.

I finally had no option except to type my own orders. After much research, I had enough information to validate my travel to Saudi Arabia as a courier. There were three senior officers who had to approve the documents. Neither one of them read the details. They all seemed distracted as I stood before them with the request for orders. I had two days to pack and get to the airport. I was going to the front lines.

All my Christians friends begged me not to go. They said if God wanted me to go, He would have sent me with everyone else. Horrible stories about living conditions came to the rear detachment. No one could believe I was foolish enough to go voluntarily. They did not understand that I *had* to go—I was on Holy Ghost orders.

I arrived in the Middle East on January 12 that year. The war was expected to officially start on January 15. When I arrived in Saudi Arabia, I praised God for His faithfulness. I distributed the ministry materials throughout the compounds and witnessed to anyone I saw. I slept in the daytime and stayed up all night, leading people to the Lord.

The Saudis set up a fried chicken hut across from the hangers where the soldiers were sleeping. Soldiers were standing in line 2-3 hours just for a bag of fried chicken. This was the perfect evangelism opportunity for me. I led many soldiers to the Lord in that chicken line in the wee hours of the morning. The day before the war started, I flew back to Germany and never returned to Saudi Arabia again.

Marriage Failure

I went to another level of intercession during Operation Desert Storm. Miracles became a norm, and I became more confident about hearing God's voice. After the war was over, my husband joined me overseas. He was a new Christian and was not filled with the Holy Spirit. Though we accepted Jesus in our lives around the same time, he was not growing in God as I was. Yet I continued to believe God for growth in his life.

Despite my prayers, things continued to get worse in our marriage. I became the victim of physical abuse, and my marriage sadly ended in divorce. As difficult and painful as this was, I chose to hold fast to God's promise to work out everything for my good, because I love Him and am called according to His purpose (Rom. 8:28).

My first marriage occurred when I did not yet know the Lord. As I stood before the county judge to say my vows, I remember feeling as though I was being inducted into the Army. In the back of my mind I was convincing myself that if it didn't work out I could get an "early release." Proper foundations are crucial for any of our endeavors, and anything built on the sand will be wiped out by the storm (Matt. 7:24-27).

God is not a man, that He should lie (Num. 23:19), but we often lie to ourselves. When we engage in this self-deception, we place our destiny in the hands of satan, the father of lies (Jn. 8:44). In contrast, God instructs us to not lean on our own understanding (Prov. 3:5).

Many times we suffer the consequences of the wrong paths we

149

have walked down. After pursuing paths that are not God's will, we often attempt to force His hand into putting a seal of approval on what we've done. Although God won't approve our wrong choices, His grace and mercy are always available to put us back on the right track. But the odds that were against my first husband and me did not disappear when I got saved.

After my divorce, I soon remarried. I can boldly say that my marriage today is strong and torments the devil. My husband and I stand as a team in God's presence and before the demonic ranks of hell. I also rejoice that my former husband is now happily married and serving the Lord.

Even today I walk out my salvation with fear and trembling. Many great men and women of God have seriously missed the mark and gotten off the track. My goal in life is to press on toward the upward call of God. There may be mistakes and setbacks, but I want to please God in the long run.

New Levels of Intimacy

One day as I was taking a bath, the presence of God filled the room. God began to speak to me like never before. He told me I would have a ministry that would be known around the world. He mentioned that I would be the steward over millions of dollars and said I would distribute money in His kingdom according to His will. The Lord was speaking so clearly that it almost seemed unreal. I had been in the bathroom approximately two hours but it seemed like only minutes.

As God was speaking, He paused and said, "You don't believe a word of what I am saying, do you?" I could not lie to God. What He spoke to me sounded so impossible. He told me that my husband had been sitting in the living room the entire time I was fellowshiping with Him. He told me to go to the living room and lay hands on him. He said that as a confirmation of His promises to me, when I laid hands on my husband, he would fall under the power of the Spirit. I obeyed the Lord, and as I touched my husband's forehead, he fell to the floor like fire. This had never happened in my home before.

As the days went by, I felt I was getting closer to God. I was addicted to spending time with God and did not want anything to interrupt my time with Him. Stealing away with my Daddy was the top priority in my life. However, I also made sure my personal and family responsibilities were in order to the best of my ability.

One night as I was walking around the house praising God, the Holy Spirit told me to kneel before Him. As I closed my eyes, the spirit realm opened up to me. I was still in my living room, but God poured anointing oil over my head from a vase. He said, "I am ordaining you to preach to the nations." God told me I was to give up my military career and move back to Jacksonville, where I was to open a center for girls on drugs. I never shared this with anyone. I never called myself a preacher or prophet. I always believed that my gift would make room for me. I knew that God ordained me in that living room and whatever happened at a later date would only be a confirmation of what He had already done.

Transitions

Before my divorce from my first husband, I was honorably discharged, because I was pregnant with my daughter, Faith. My husband did not want to move back to the United States because God had not spoken to him. I did everything within my power to obey God and trusted that He would touch my husband's heart. Despite the disagreement, the peace of God surrounded my mind. Even though the Lord had told me to move back to Jacksonville, I finally came in agreement with my husband to extend our tour overseas. I was waiting on God to touch my husband's heart.

A decision had to be made because my husband's enlistment period was soon up. I had always been good at getting military documents completed and approved, but this time there was some kind of blockage operating. We seemed to be stuck in limbo. We never got a response from my husband's superiors.

After a while, I decided to call my husband's commanding officer to find out why we were not getting any responses. Her response took my breath away, as she informed me that my husband had been barred from reenlistment for two years. I could not believe my ears. How could the person I trusted keep such a thing from me? I had given up my military career, and in two months we would *both* be without jobs. He had known that he could not reenlist for two years, yet he led me on as if it were a game.

I never understood why this happened, but I knew I had to believe God for provision. I had a three-month-old baby, and it was no time for doubt. The Bible says that all things work out for the good of those who love the Lord and are called according to His purpose (Rom. 8:28). The good that came out of what seemed to be a horrible situation was that I was going back to Florida, where God had already told me I should be.

As I flew home on the plane, the Holy Spirit comforted me. I will never forget His words to me that day: "I will show myself mighty among men on your behalf. Houses, finances and land shall be of no concern, for I shall provide all you need." From that day to this, I have never been late on a mortgage, car note or light bill.

Chapter 17
MINISTRY ASSIGNMENT

Florida was as beautiful as ever. I enjoyed my time with God when I was overseas, but Germany always seemed to have a dreary, gray overcast feel to it. I was so excited to be home, and I started a secular career as a social worker in the food stamp office. We were overworked and underpaid, but I delighted in being in the midst of so many lost souls.

I worked at the Goodwin Branch, only 10 minutes from uptown, so I was like a fish in water. Every day there was someone threatening to shoot up the building because they did not get their food stamps. Most of the staff was nervous, but the excitement always put a smile on my face. I would come out and talk street talk and take people back into my office and help them.

Mr. Averly was the district director, and he made a special position for me to handle all the "problem" cases. No one said anything to me about praying for people or ministering on the job. Although some of my co-workers complained about having a college education and yet working under the conditions we faced, I praised God because I knew He had placed me there.

I attended church with Pastor Bea and Sirretta, and we went to the streets as much as we could. I requested a meeting with my pastor to share the vision God had given me. To my disappointment, he asked that I wait two years before opening the drug rehab center for women. In contrast, both of my pastors in Germany had released me, saying they supported what God had told me to do.

I submitted to the pastor's request, but for the next month I literally felt as if I had backslidden. It was difficult for me to even get out of bed for church. I loved my pastor so much, but my obedience to him was placing my soul in trouble. I wasn't a "Lone Ranger," but sincerely wanted to start the center under his covering and supervision. I know he meant well and probably thought I was too young in the Lord. He didn't know me very well and hadn't seen how the Lord used me overseas.

Obeying God Rather Than Men

Finally I told my pastor that I had to obey God in opening the drug rehab center. He told me that my ministry would be a bastard ministry. He also said that his ministry had proven itself and that my ministry would have to do the same thing. The respect that I had for him as the anointed of God far outweighed the words that came from his mouth that day. My love for him was unconditional, and I realized he simply didn't understand how the Lord was leading me. Despite his objections, God's vision had to go on.

How do you start a drug rehab center with no manpower, materials or financial support? The Holy Spirit led me step by step, and He supernaturally provided all along the way. The first step was getting a building. I prayed for months for a building, and nothing seemed to come available. All my co-workers at the food stamp office knew about my vision for the center, for it was all I talked about. The name would be "Spoken Word Center I," because there would be many other centers to follow.

One day as I shared the vision of the building with one of my co-workers, I determined in my heart that I was going to leave work on my lunch break and not return until I had found a suitable building. That day I had a 1½ hour lunch break, for I had made up my mind that I would rather get fired than return to work without a building. I got in my van and prayed in tongues. Within 20 minutes I was in a neighborhood I was not familiar with. I found myself signing a contract for the first house I looked at. It was perfect. Though this two-bedroom wooden house needed a lot of work, it looked like an elegant resort to me. God was faithful.

An Unlikely Worship Leader

For four months I just paid the note on the building. I was attending a Baptist church where they allowed me to teach and lead praise and worship. Being a worship leader was something new to me. There was a time when Sirretta and I backed up Pastor Bea when she led worship, but all we did was just move our lips. Our voices were terrible!

How could I now lead a praise service? It's an interesting story. During my ordination service, a female pastor was in charge. She operated under a heavy prophetic anointing. She stood before me and began to laugh uncontrollably. I knew the spirit of God was on her, but I did not understand what He was trying to say. An ordination should be a serious, solemn moment. Why was this woman laughing? Finally, the Lord spoke through her and said, "I shall have the last laugh, for you shall sing under the anointing!"

I then understood why she was laughing, because my voice was so bad the very thought of me singing was a joke. People had criticized my voice for so long, the fulfillment of this prophetic word would truly have to be God. At that moment a woman who sang beautifully during the praise service stepped out and put two fingers on my throat as she sang a note that could have shattered glass. I received the word by faith and did not think twice about it.

Approximately a month later, I was preparing to minister at a female correctional facility, and all my singers were canceling out. By this time Spoken Word Center was known throughout the city, and I had many ministry associates. The best singers in town would travel with our outreach ministry. I would preach and they would minister in song. I would spend an entire morning with the inmates and teach them skits to put on for the general population. We became known as "Smoking Word Ministries" behind prison walls, because they could tell we had the fire of God.

On this particular trip all the singers had other engagements. I felt as if we had to have at least one song, even if I had to sing it myself. I picked up my stepmother and best friend and told them I was going to sing. They laughed and made jokes like, "What key do you sing in?" and "Are you a soprano or alto?" I did not know anything about keys or sopranos. All I knew is that those women needed to be ministered to in song.

As I put the microphone to my mouth before 200 inmates, my knees shook and my two armorbearers had tears running down their faces to keep from bursting out laughing. I did not care what they thought; I had to at least try. I only knew one song and it was "I'll Never Give Up On You." As I opened my mouth to sing, my stepmother and friend stopped laughing and their eyes got big. I was sounding good! They could not believe what was coming out of my mouth, and neither could I. I was singing not just from my vocal cords, but from my heart. Glory to God, the Lord had anointed me to sing. The devil has ridiculed my voice for 30 years, and now I would torment him by singing praise songs to Jesus. Today, as I write this book, my first praise CD is being released. To God be the glory!

Victories at the Center

Spoken Word Center won the Family In Action Award for substance abuse rehab. I became well known in the city, both in the ministry and the secular arenas. We housed, clothed and fed up to 15 young ladies at a time.

Sirretta and I managed the center with very little support. Few churches gave donations, and the ones that invited us to do services usually received big offerings but only gave us a few dollars. Even with these adverse circumstances, we lived in abundance. When I was in Germany I attended Mighty In Spirit Bible Institute, under the leadership of Reverend Billy Godwin. He insisted that we read biographies of great men and women in ministry. I loved reading about Smith Wigglesworth and other mighty saints.

One of our mandatory books was about a man named George Mueller. I thought Brother Billy had really missed God by making us read this book. There were no legs growing out or no one was being raised from the dead. How boring! It was basically a journal of how God provided supernaturally to feed the children in the orphanage on a daily basis. When I was given the responsibility to feed up to 15 ex-prostitutes with no help from the government, I often thought about Mueller's testimony. The book that once seemed so boring became a very important part of my life.

Not only did God provide our daily bread, but He did so in abundance. Yet He always kept us in a place to pray. We had to believe Him for everything we got. Grant after grant was turned down, but we never went without. God blessed us with two duplexes that were side by side. They were freshly renovated and very beautiful, but the surrounding neighborhood was hardcore. A group of transvestites lived across the street.

The young ladies who came to our ministry were not exactly princesses from a storybook. They were robbers, murderers, prostitutes, con artists and even AIDS victims. We received girls who looked like they were scraped off the sidewalk and dropped on our porch. Sirretta would tend their sores and nurse them back to health.

When it was becoming increasingly difficult for us to transport these young ladies to other churches, God spoke to my heart that I was to pastor them. After a few weeks, they went from a mess to a miracle. Some of them could sing like angels and some could preach better than me.

We had so much fun in the center. We had ladies healed from AIDS, families restored and lives transformed. One of our favorite sayings was, "Girl, it is sho nuf real!" God gave me a "confession of faith" that the ladies memorized and spoke into their own lives daily. Today we speak that confession in every service at Spoken Word.

Lisa's Story

Soon we formed a singing group called the "Voices of Deliverance." When these ladies sang, the demons trembled. One young lady stood out above the rest. Her name was Lisa, and she had charisma. When she picked up the microphone, the anointing fell. She had problems with a bad attitude and a foul mouth, but Sirretta and I had no problem dealing with it. Lisa's testimony was that she had escaped from a serial killer who had been killing prostitutes in our city. Whenever she told her story, the power of God took over the place.

However, Lisa struggled with temptation and went back and forth into the world. For some reason she could not get rooted in God. I had a particular love for her, because I could see that she was much like me before I was saved. Lisa could not disconnect from the streets and left the ministry for two years.

One day God laid her on my heart, and I went on the streets looking for her. She typically walked a particular corner off of Main Street, and that's where I found her. She looked like a sack of bones with a T-shirt on. The devil had clouded her mind to such an extent that she did not have any pants on except underwear. She addressed me very disrespectfully, something she had never done before.

The Spirit of God came on me and I prophesied to her that she had two weeks to come back to God. Two weeks later I was preaching at her funeral. It was one of the hardest things I have ever done.

Lisa was killed while prostituting and doing crack. Word on the streets was that she was murdered by the same man she had escaped from the first time. I could only question what would make a person knowingly step into the same death trap. All that rose up in my spirit was, "Either we live by our testimony, or we die by it!"

Chapter 18
STRAINED RELATIONSHIPS

I was in covenant with several other ministries in the Jacksonville area, and every time they had a program, I was invited. God was opening doors for me to preach throughout the state of Florida. The income from my evangelistic trips supported the drug rehab center.

While I was ministering in a nearby city, a prophet of God walked up to me and said, "Snakes are all around you, God is about to pull you out of the clique!" Two weeks later a popular evangelist told me these words, "Yea, you little dreamer, your brothers and sisters are about to throw you in a pit and leave you for dead!" The Bible says, "Out of the mouth of two or three witnesses, let every word be established," so I took these words seriously.

I have not said much about my first husband, because I have since then been divorced and remarried. My first husband stood with me as a support in the public, but his heart was not for street people. He would often refer to them with derogatory names that made me want to cry. He also ridiculed me for hanging out with "them people."

To my amazement, I soon found out that most of the ministers I knew felt the same way. They were often suspicious of me because of the ladies at the center. Some of them even suspected that I was a homosexual. I was approached many times by local ministers about "spiritual do's and don'ts." As long as I followed their counsel, they tolerated me. When I dared to be different, they backed away or placed restrictions on my relationship with them. This was painful, for I had a great desire to be accepted by other ministers.

God led me to continue my studies at a local Bible college. I was so excited that I recruited four other pastors. I looked forward to those nights of fellowship, and I took the girls from the center with me. Many other pastors from around the city were in attendance, and I was glad to be a part of it.

One of the people I invited to be a part of the Bible college was Jessica, who was one of my best friends. She had moved to Florida from Germany to become a part of Spoken Word, and she was my assistant at the church. God had used her to minister to me when I was a new believer.

At the Bible college they had nights when they allowed one of the area pastors to speak for 10-15 minutes. As the weeks went by, it became very obvious that I was the only pastor who was not invited to speak. Instead of asking me to speak, they put Jessica in the pulpit. Even though I was not anxious to do anything God hadn't called me to do, I knew something was not right about what they were doing. I could see that they did not respect me as a pastor and that they thought Jessica should not be in a ministry like mine. In their eyes I had become one of "those people" that my husband talked about.

As distressing as this situation was, God kept me from any deep-rooted backlash from this. As I stood in the Bible college one day, the Holy Spirit spoke expressly: "They are trying to hold you down, but this is My perfect will. Your flesh must be held down and you must humble yourself. This must happen in order for your ministry to come forth as I have planned. As they hold you down, I will rise up. Always remember: They can never hold Me down." After hearing this word from the Lord, the situation became a piece of cake. I had an even greater love for everyone involved, because I knew I was in God's will.

Starting Over

When my first marriage ended in divorce, my relationships were hindered with many of my Christian friends. This was not made any better by the fact that I got married to my present husband not long after my divorce. Local pastors disassociated themselves with me, and several families in my church scattered. Satan was laughing at me, but he did not understand that all things were working out for my good.

My family was not as much upset with my divorce as they were with whom I was marrying. Danny was the same man who had left me 12 years before to marry another woman. When God said Danny was to be my husband, I began to bind the devil. I never felt that Danny could sell out to God. Yet how quickly I had forgotten that if God could save and deliver a wretch like me, He could do it for Danny!

Cocaine killed our first baby, but today we have identical twins, Elijah and Elisha. We also have four kids between us from previous marriages. The Lord has blessed us to have an effective deliverance ministry as a team. And the thing that excites me the most is the anointing God has placed on our marriage ministry.

By God's grace and mercy, Danny and I have both made it through the ugly blemishes of divorce. Today we stand delivered from it all. God's best for His children is to be equally yoked and never have to look the demon of divorce in its ugly face. Even as I write this book, I know that the enemy would like to sift my marriage like wheat. But my marriage is a testimony to the power of God, and truly, "What God has joined together, let no man put asunder." I encourage those of you who have been through the trauma of broken marriages that there is life after divorce. If God can deliver you from drugs, AIDS and all kinds of other terrible situations, He can deliver you from the scars of a failed marriage.

Even though I had only been in ministry for a few years, after my divorce I found myself starting all over again. The Church of God took me under its wing as a pastor. I'm sure I was quite different from most of the ministers in their organization, and they seemed strange to me. Despite our differences, they allowed me to minister throughout the state of Florida. I would cast out devils and pray for people to be filled with the Holy Spirit without any hindrances.

Bishop Wallace Sibley and Bishop Quan Miller are still my overseers. God put a special place in my heart for them, because they did the one thing that meant the most to me: They allowed me to preach the gospel freely! One spring I was invited to teach at a women's statewide meeting. My assignment was to do a workshop, and I had never before spoken to a crowd of that size up.

My title was "From a Mess to a Miracle," and I was scheduled to do two sessions. The first session went so well they had to move me to a larger room. I was so nervous that I could hardly breathe. As they moved me to the larger room, crowds of women were outside the doors, demanding entrance. A lady looked at me and said, "Have you heard this lady speak?!" For a minute, I did not even know who she was referring to. They were talking about me!

National evangelists were speaking at this meeting, but everyone was in an uproar about the young girl who preached on the subject, "From a Mess to a Miracle." The last session was so crowded that people were on the walls and floors.

They appeared happy just to be in the room. Many had been turned away, and the fire department came and made some of the women leave the session because of building codes. I could see that God's seal of approval was upon my head, and ladies still approach me today about that meeting.

Ministry Back Home

Even though my ministry was becoming increasingly popular throughout the state of Florida, things seemed to be standing still with the ministry in my hometown. I remember sitting in a building that seated 900 with fewer than 20 people in our service. On Easter Sunday most churches have lots of visitors, but I saw two Easter Sundays pass by with no one coming to our services except the "faithful few." Whenever I started to get discouraged, though, the Lord would encourage me with a dream or vision.

Spoken Word Ministries was not always popular in the church realm, but we definitely drew attention on the dark side. We could honestly say that the demons knew who were. Witches, warlocks and other occult members began to approach me for help. They often said they wanted to be delivered but were afraid that God could not offer the protection they needed from satan if they left him. After these people contacted me, the demons would often torment them and keep them away from me.

I made up my mind that if I were never known in the church world, at least hell would know me! In the Bible the demons exclaimed, *"Jesus I know, and Paul I know; but who are you?"* (Acts 19:15) The reason that the demons recognize you is because God recognizes you. I had been rejected by the local church and delivered from the religious clique, but through it all I grew closer to God and more focused on His vision for my life.

I could see no increase in the natural realm but I had an eye in the spirit and could see my promise. God was not a man, that He should lie (Num. 23:19). I chose to believe Him no matter what my circumstances said. Every month around bill time, I had to shut myself in my prayer closet and pray for provision. Sometimes I would put the bills under my feet, and at other times I would tie them around my waist. But every time God would supernaturally provide. He was never late!

Curses of Death

On a beautiful Sunday morning, I received a call on my pager from a strange man. He said he was from a group called the "Eifi." He told me he was studying to be a voodoo priest and had been watching me. The group he did witchcraft with had been sending curses to kill Pastor Bea and myself. He told me he was trying to come out of the voodoo cult, and encouraged me to keep doing what I was doing, because their curses could not touch Pastor Bea or me. Despite his involvement in the dark side, he told me, "You are on the right track!"

I informed Pastor Bea about the warning, but she did not seem to take me seriously. Although we talked periodically, Pastor Bea had pretty much discontinued socializing with me by this time. We had churches within a few blocks of each other, but we seldom fellowshiped. I always respected her and was grateful for what she had taught Sirretta and me about casting out devils, but it was time for me to go to the next level.

The weapons of witchcraft started manifesting themselves against us in our local church. The Bible says that even though weapons may be formed against us and may manifest, they shall not prosper. Witches and warlocks started disrupting our services with bizarre outbursts. We also soon learned about "empty shells," which is what we called people who had no natural motives against us, but who would manifest as our enemies.

The devil would knock them out and use them against us to disturb our services. We often had to call the police to physically escort them out.

Dead animals and pennies that had been cursed started being found around the building. The pennies had been cursed with poverty demons that were supposed to impoverish those who picked them up.

Learning from the Enemy

By this time we had 30-40 people, and everyone was from the streets. We had jack men, street women, and con artists who were all saved, delivered and filled with the Holy Ghost. We were in a battle that we did not understand, but God had a surprise for us: He sent us helpful reinforcements from the other side.

During a marriage counseling session, my husband and I felt led to invite a particular young couple to our home. Keith and Lynn were very strange and we knew there were walls around them that had to come down. One night Lynn called me off to the side and shared that she had been a "white witch." She explained that she was a member of the Yoruba Religion and that Eli was her BaBa (high priest) and Cheryl was her high priestess.

My mouth dropped, and I could not find words to respond. Lynn said that before coming to our ministry she was on her way to be buried with dead body parts in a casket in Yoruba Village in the Carolinas. She had built an altar in her living room to worship her ancestors and Keith was a "worshiper" of crack cocaine. She explained some of the orishas (gods) that she served:

> **Obatala** - god of marijuana
> **Ogon/Oshun** - road gods that cause people to have
>   accidents as witches feed them sacrifices
> **Shango** - god of guns and knives.

167

The Yoruba religion is the same as the Santeria religion, which is the same as the group called Eifi. The only distinction is race, for Santeria originates from the Spanish community and Yoruba is practice by the black race. The gods (orishas) are very similar and even have the same names. With these is mixed a strange blend of Catholicism and voodoo. This religion masks itself through culture and fads that bewitch the ignorant.

Lynn explained to me that through the use of chants, rituals and her personal demon, she could get anything she wanted. Some examples of the demonic fads and fetishes of the Yoruba religion are:

> **Egun Egun Sticks** - Sticks that have strange carvings and may resemble a totem pole. They are disguised as walking sticks but are used to hit the ground and call up ancestral gods.

> **Ju-Ju Bags** - Draw bags that are small and usually worn around the waist. They look like the bags liquor is sold in. The purpose of the bags is to catch spirits and supposedly protect people. They are a type of charm or talisman.

Over the next year, my husband and I became very close to Keith and Lynn, the Yoruba couple who eventually were saved and delivered. They taught us a lot about the dark side, and we used it as secret intelligence against the enemy. I started meeting demons face-to-face and encountering bizarre dreams and vision. My husband and I knew that God had a purpose in allowing us to go through these experiences, but we didn't have the slightest idea what the purpose was. All we knew was that we wanted God's will to be done, not ours.

I began having a series of dreams. I would receive one part of the dream and then have the second part come on another night.

In the dreams, men were always after me. I would fight, resist and even run. Sometimes I would run so fast that my feet would leave the ground and I would begin to fly. Although I would ultimately escape, the men would always hold my family captive. When I reached a phone, I would pick it up and dial "911." The operator always said, "This is directory assistance, may I help you please?" I was so frustrated. I kept dialing 911, but I was reaching 411. I knew I didn't need information—I needed help!

God revealed to me that people were coming to the church with critical situations that needed to be policed. Police exercise the authority of the law. Instead of getting the police, they were merely getting information. Paul clearly stated that the kingdom of God was not only in "word" (information), but also in power. We need the word of faith, but faith without works is dead.

For too long, we have merely been telling people they can be delivered. God is now sending forth a generation of soldiers who will manifest His power in the earthly realm. I will never forget the frustration of that dream. I did not want information; I needed someone with the authority to make those men release my family.

God has given us authority over all the power of the enemy. But unused spiritual power is like a lamp with the plug pulled out of the socket. When a born-again believer plugs into the power of the Holy Spirit, satan must release what is theirs. I decided that I wanted to teach people to do the greater works, no matter what the cost. But my natural mind could not fathom the warfare I was about to encounter.

Chapter 19
ORDAINED—
AND ACTIVATED

Lynn and I were featured on a local Christian television program, and I exposed a demon called Pan, which is the god of panic. The word "pandemonium," which means the capital of hell, is derived from the root word *pan*. Pan is also the god that presides over Greek sororities and fraternities. All sororities and fraternities come under the covering of the Pan Hellenic Council.

After I exposed this demon, the uproar was so great that the station manger barred me from speaking over the air again. One of my church members worked at the station and heard and heard the manager say, "Who pulled *her* from under a rock?" And this guy was absolutely right: I not only came from under *a* rock, I came from under *the* Rock—Jesus!

The incident at the Christian television station was just another indication that the truth I preached seemed foreign to most believers. I had taken many arrows in my city, but God gave me a peace concerning the television incident. He told me that one day I would be able to preach the unadulterated truth on any station I desired. Although the word of the Lord seemed very clear on this, it certainly looked impossible in the natural. Instead of allowing the response of the station manager to sidetrack me, I just shifted my faith forward another gear and went on in the Holy Ghost.

By this time I had personally met demons face-to-face. I would hear their names in the spirit, and God would also direct me to do extensive research. Names like *Poltergeist, Lilith* and *Cockatrice* became part of my everyday vocabulary. I had met Succubus face-to-face on several occasions, and God gave me many revelations concerning this spirit. I had never read a book to describe such spirits, but my knowledge came mainly through dreams, visions or deliverance encounters. The unseen realm became as real to me as the people I saw every day.

New Prosperity

Over the years, God has always dealt with me concerning giving. One night He pulled me aside and told me there would be no more stomping on bills or putting them around my waist. He said clearly, "No more month-to-month faith." Not only did God want me to believe Him to be debt-free, but He also wanted me to increase my giving to a whole new level.

I had seldom watched Pastor Rod Parsley on television, but God prompted me to plant a seed into his ministry. I was instructed to get two prayer cloths, something I had never done before. God told to put one cloth under my mattress and the other under my pulpit. After my obedience, our congregation quickly grew to one hundred members in only two months. From that time to now, our ministry's financial status has been just as God had spoken: abundant provision.

The Lord also told me to purchase a very expensive 30-foot recreation vehicle (RV). Just about everyone I knew criticized me for purchasing this vehicle. I was instructed to call it my Demon- Buster Mobile and use it for evangelism. No one seemed to be able to catch the vision, but God had spoken to me. We were a few thousand dollars from purchasing the vehicle, when God told me to plant another seed in Pastor Parsley's ministry. This time I was directed to personally deliver it.

God's instruction was clear on this, but the provision was a little foggy. The Lord also said that Pastor Parsley would ordain me. How could this be? I did not know where to start, but God provided for us to attend the World Harvest Pastors Conference. As we walked in the door, Pastor Parsley was on the screen asking all pastors who were to be ordained to come forward. I looked at my husband and said, "That's us!" We immediately went into the sanctuary and stood in the front of the altar with the other pastors who were to be ordained.

As Pastor Parsley came down the prayer line, he laid hands on us and we fell under the power of God. With everything within me, I knew we were in the Lord's perfect will. As the word of the Lord was going forth in power, the Holy Spirit quietly spoke to me and said, "Go to the bonfire area." When we got to the bonfire area, a well-dressed man greeted us and began to talk with us. I shared with him that I had been ordained by Pastor Parsley and was a part of the ministerial alliance.

The man looked at me with a puzzled face, because he was the director of that department and did not recognize my name. I smiled and comforted him, letting him know that God told me to walk down that aisle and it would work out for good. The gentleman took me and gave me the paperwork that had to be completed for ordination and to become a member of the fellowship. Religion would say I was out of order, but those who have a relationship with God understand that He will take the foolish things to confound the wise. A month later I was officially accepted into the ministerial alliance, but I knew that an impartation had already taken place.

Within five months after Pastor Parsley laid hands on my husband and me, doors were opened that released Spoken Word Ministries to the nations. I recently had dinner with Pastor Parsley and shared our testimony with him about the supernatural ordination and impartation we received at that pastors conference. He laughed as he leaned back in his chair, and actually thought it was quite a testimony. Pastor Parsley even sent his camera crew to our church and home in order to record our testimony. If God leads you into a situation, He covers all the bases.

Learning Obedience

The ordination service was not the only thing God used to change my life and my ministry. It was actually a part of a series of events that required uncompromising obedience to God. So many people have their own plans as to how God will bring about the great breakthrough they have been waiting for. I must admit that I have been guilty of the same attitude myself.

The most dangerous thing believers can do is put their hopes in particular situations or events. When we do this, we put God in a box and open doors to spirits of disappointment and doubt. If I had to give a formula for breakthroughs and being in God's perfect will, it would be five words: "Obedience is better than sacrifice!"

Six months before I met Dr. C. Peter Wagner, God brought about several experiences that changed my life. The first incident occurred at the Church of God state conference in Florida. One of my pastors and I were attending a series of meetings that were going along very well. I was enjoying the fact that I was not ministering but had the opportunity to be ministered to for three days. In the middle of the daytime seminar, the Holy Spirit prompted me to get something to eat. I was not very hungry, but the urge to go to the restaurant became very strong. When I presented the idea, Pastor Turner looked at me like I was crazy, for it did not make sense to leave in the middle of a meeting in order to get something to eat.

Despite Pastor Turner's reaction, I soon had to leave the service, because I couldn't get my mind off the restaurant. I joked with Pastor Turner that maybe we had backslidden. The next ironic thing was that the only restaurant in the conference area was a lounge that had a big crowd drinking alcoholic beverages. I did not understand what was happening, so I ordered a sandwich to go, even though I had no desire to eat it. Pastor Turner and I laughed all the way back to the conference hall about an episode we thought wasn't very spiritual.

The laughing ceased as we saw a middle-aged man trying to jump off of the bridge we were walking across. We physically stopped him from jumping, and then began to minister to him. After we calmed him down and led him in the sinner's prayer, he told us how hungry he was. Praise the Lord, I had a freshly cooked Reuben sandwich and a drink in my bag! All of a sudden the situation that seemed so unspiritual had become a great testimony.

My heart filled with compassion as the suicidal homeless man shared with me how he was begging for food and someone had given him a sandwich with a rock in it. When he bit into the sandwich, one of his teeth came out. His mouth was still bloody from the incident. He had just been kicked out of the lounge where we got the sandwich, and he felt that life was not worth it anymore. He told the people who kicked him out that Jesus loved him, but they only mocked him in return.

After confirming that Jesus really did love him, we went back to the conference. As I walked across the remainder of the bridge, I pondered how many people had crossed the bridge that day, but God chose us to save a life. When we returned to the meeting, the auditorium was packed. Bishops from around the country were present. I was enjoying the preaching, and the music in the background enhanced the moment. God came on me in a special way, and it seemed as if the Holy Spirit was tickling me. At my seat, I fell under the power of God three or four times.

When I stood up, a tickling sensation shot throughout my body. The thing that made this occurrence so strange is that no one else was responding this way. Then the word of the Lord came to me, saying, "Run around the building!" I was not anxious to run around a crowd of three thousand people, with bishops lined across the front stage. Yet God continued to bid me to run. Finally the Spirit said, "If you run, I will tear down strongholds!"

On those words, I ran as fast as I could. I had a long, flowing dress on, so I gathered it up to my knees and ran like a wild woman. My bishop said that I ran by the podium so fast that he could not tell it was me. At the completion of my run, I fell under the power of the Spirit, and God began to speak to me. He said that next year at this time, the people would say, "This is why she was running." This meeting was held in June 1998, and in July 1999; I was speaking at the National Congress on Deliverance, hosted by Dr. C. Peter Wagner.

The Demon-Buster Mobile

The next act of obedience God required of me was to purchase a $60,000 recreation vehicle, as I mentioned before. He told me to call it the Demon-Buster Mobile. People laughed at this idea, just as they laughed at me running around that huge auditorium like a wild woman. Even my closet advisors did not agree that such a vehicle was necessary. I did not even know what to do with it when I got it, but I knew I had to obey God at any cost.

God supernaturally allowed us to drive that brand new vehicle off the lot. I would not let anyone see it until I had put the words "Demon-Buster Mobile" on it. We used the vehicle for street evangelism, and it really got people's attention. The first time we put it on the road was to see Bob Larson, a deliverance minister, in central Florida. We could not find a place to park, so I proudly parked it in front of the church. Devil worshipers filled the church that day, for they often follow Bob Larson's ministry around. They dress in black "witchcraft drag," paint their faces, and even have voodoo dolls and posters of Bob Larson.

I had never been so excited in my life. The meeting went well, and I even interviewed a few devil worshipers. We were waiting outside in the Demon-Buster Mobile, and a long train of cars with police escort pulled up on the side of us. Two men stepped out of a vehicle and knocked on the door of the RV. It was Bob Larson and one of Dr. Billy Graham's associates. My heart was beating so fast I could hardly catch my breath. Mr. Larson said he only wanted to know who was crazy enough to have a vehicle like that. Before leaving with his entourage, he invited me to be on his radio broadcast. I thought it was very nice of him to have me on his radio broadcast and thanked God for the opportunity.

New Doors Opening

1998 was almost gone. At the end of each year, God has always spoken great things to me about my future ministry. I had a big vision and always knew I was called to do more than what I was presently doing, even though I had little support or finances. The word of the Lord to me this particular December was, "At the beginning of the year to come, I shall put you in the company of those who are considered to be giants in the ministry, and they shall be drawn by the genuineness of your faith." Like every other year, I received the word of the Lord and pressed toward it. I did not realize that this time God's "beginning of the year" lined up with mine.

Everyone has great expectations of God when He says, "By this time tomorrow" (see 2 Kin. 7:1). The problem is, our tomorrow never lines up with His. God has recently revealed to me that one of the main reasons our ways and thoughts are not like His is because we are subject to time. Before Adam and Eve sinned, time was never an issue. Their biological clock started ticking as a result of the curse.

By the middle of January, I received a letter from Mission America about a group of ministers meeting to discuss deliverance issues in the nation. The names on the list were those I had only seen on television and in bookstores. I knew I had to make this trip. It was not until a week later that I realized my name was listed as a pastor with this group. Concerned that they had made a mistake, I called to see if they had the right Kim Daniels. Indeed, I was the right one.

Who could have recommended me? I found out later that Bob Larson had recommended "the lady with the Demon-Buster Mobile." God truly takes the foolish things to confound the wise. In the meeting I was invited to, I met Dr. C. Peter Wagner, Chuck Pierce and many other great men and women of God in the Spiritual Warfare Network. My message to them is the same one I present to you today: Warfare and deliverance require a high level of discipline and obedience to God.

Everyone treated me well at that meeting, but the highlight was when Dr. Wagner told Chuck Pierce, "Kim will speak at the Congress on Deliverance!" My tomorrow had finally lined up with God's. My response to Dr. Wagner's decision was that I had never seen such great faith in all the land. Peter and Doris Wagner had never heard me minister and knew nothing about my lifestyle. They only followed the unction of the Holy Spirit.

As I have become acquainted with Dr. Wagner's ministry, I have discovered that he has been known to take on a challenge. By asking me to speak at the 1999 Congress on Deliverance, he really launched out into the deep. The outcome of this story is that all of heaven backed him up!

This is the kind of people I want to be surrounded by: Spirit-led saints. These are people who do not seek occasion or position, but seek the face of the Father, desiring to do His will in the earthly realm.

Thank you for taking the time to read my story.

Epilogue
A FINAL CHALLENGE

Spiritual warfare ministries that expose the plots and plans of the enemy will always be highly targeted by the hordes of hell. I have personally witnessed pioneers operating on this level being torn down and branded as heretics by their own brothers and sisters in the Lord. If what we know is not undergirded with intercession and covered with the blood of Jesus, it will cause an even greater destruction.

Many will not admit it, but "knowledge is power!" The enemy's power operates fluently through deception, trying to keep people blinded by what is really going on. The United States and other countries have secret intelligence agents who operate under-cover to gather pertinent information from enemy armed forces. The CIA and FBI are far more powerful than the law enforce-ment officers or military personnel who wear uniforms.

The resources of these agencies are mind-boggling to regular citizen, but those who have inside information are able to understand the amazing effectiveness of these operations. It would be hard for most regular citizens to believe some of the things that are actually taking place in our government, cities and neighborhoods in the United States of America. There are even top-secret projects that most military personnel and law officials would have a hard time believing.

Spoken Word Ministries is a secret intelligence unit for the Lord in the body of Christ. Some of the revelations and teachings we share may be difficult even for those who have been in the Word of the Lord for many years. I believe that the enemy has loosed a tongue-tying spirit against many men and women of God, causing them to neglect speaking the whole truth. Most of the things that we teach have been revealed to many others, but often they choose not to deal with the pressure of telling the "whole truth."

The Bible says there will be a season in the last days when people of God will not be able to endure sound doctrine. People will not be able to proclaim sound doctrine because of the persecution that comes with it. There are secret agencies that have been strategically put in place to release the will of the antichrist spirit in the earthly realm. These demonic organizations are mixed with natural and supernatural powers, with a goal to control the world. The powers are both terrestrial and celestial in nature, but work hand-in-hand to do satan's will.

God has shown me that this is the end-time "spirit of the agent." As this book is reaching your hands, they are devising a plan to destroy and discredit Spoken Word Ministries and everything this book stands for. If they cannot sabotage or entrap God's elect, they will simply make up a lie. The sad part about this is that there are those in the church who will sooner believe a lie than believe the truth.

The Bible says that before Stephen was stoned the religious sects tried to find fault in what he was teaching. He taught with such power and revelation that his words could not be denied. When they could not find fault in what he was teaching, they coerced people to lie about him and accuse him of heresy. We have to be very careful not to pick up stones and cast them at our brothers and sisters who are of another fold.

Sometimes we can become so mingled with the world that sound doctrine will become heresy in our eyes. Quality time with God is the only thing that sharpens spiritual discernment. We must be spiritually in a place to try the spirits of these last days as to whether they are of God or not. Revealed truth is the greatest weapon we have against the forces of the evil one. When we receive the truth of God's Word in its entirety, we strip satan's forces of their ammunition. On the other hand, when the truth is neglected or rejected, either in whole or in part, the gates of hell can and will inflict damage against God's people.

If we are not rooted and grounded in spiritual truth, we become targets for seduction. In 1 Timothy 4:1 the Spirit speaks expressly that in the latter times some will fall away from the faith, giving heed to seducing spirits and doctrines of demons. When preachers omit the foundational teaching of deliverance and spiritual warfare from the diets of their flock, the people become deficient in their understanding of the whole truth.

This is a perfect example of spiritual neglect, and the ultimate end is the perverting of the gospel. To pervert means to misuse or take something off the original course of its purpose, which makes it entirely wrong. A half-truth is a doctrine of devils. The vision of this book and my testimony is to tell the whole truth and expose the devil's hidden snares. These snares have been suctioning the people's souls into the pit of hell through lying and seducing spirits.

I cannot do it alone. I need your prayers and support. The Bible says that iron sharpens iron. This means that the soldiers of the Lord who are on the front lines need to hear "amen" from their rear support. The word "amen" means, "I trust that what you are saying is true." Once we grasp the truth and hold on to it, no lying spirit from hell can penetrate the power of it. We must stand back to back against the accuser of the brethren and let him know that we are the true bride of Christ. Let us join forces as the body of Christ to expose and defeat the hordes of hell. We must occupy until Jesus comes…until then, let us destroy the works of the devil!